Louis Dudek (1918–)

TERRY GOLDIE

Biography

LOUIS DUDEK was born on 6 February 1918 in Montreal, the city where his activities as poet, critic, and editor have always centred. As Ralph Gustafson succinctly puts it,

> Louis Dudek was born in Montreal; lives in Montreal; always returns to the harbour of his birthright and local knowledge.[1]

Both his parents were of Polish descent, though his father had been born in Russia, his mother in England. They met and married in Canada and had three children, Louis and two daughters.

From an early age, Dudek was interested in poetry. Wynne Francis records that at fifteen he engaged in a poetry competition with his sister and was judged the victor by his parish priest.[2] Whether or not he felt this proved his ability, it is an event he has recalled more than once. Several other factors in Dudek's youth seem to be relevant to his later development. His father had various labouring jobs, in which he was often held back by poor English. This experience of economic hardship and social disadvantage shaped Dudek's early concern for the working class. The linguistic environment in Dudek's home, Polish with a growing presence of English, may have sown the seed for Dudek's lifelong interest in bilingualism and multilingualism.

Dudek's mother died in 1926, and an aunt was brought out from Poland to look after the children. The psychological effects of this change on an eight-year-old must have been major, though any theories about their specific nature can only be speculative. Still, Susan Stromberg-Stein suggests they included a strong influence on Dudek's poetic sensibility.[3]

As a youth, Dudek clung very closely to his Roman Catholic origins. He broke with the religion in his late teens but has never turned to the strident opposition to it which might be expected: "I'm not an anti-Catholic. I'm a lapsed Catholic. Be a believer in what you know. Life is a myriad-sided existence. Believe in it."[4] Wynne Francis provides the following analysis:

> Growing up in a working-class milieu during the Depression years, Dudek came to believe that religion was incapable of measuring the complexities of modern life, that it took inadequate account of both the beauty and the horror of natural existence, and that it was restrictive and inhibiting in its view of mankind. Poetry on the other hand offered an increasingly appealing way of assessing life. (p. 7)

During 1936–39 Dudek attended McGill University, where he became an associate editor of *The McGill Daily*, the first of many editing roles he has had. After graduation, he supported himself by freelancing as a journalist and advertising copywriter, though he continued to publish poetry in the *Daily* and to associate with its staff. In 1940 he met another young poet, Irving Layton; and in 1942 Layton introduced him to John Sutherland, who had just begun a new little magazine, *First Statement*. Dudek has always emphasized the limitations of his involvement with the magazine, but his position on the editorial board and his contributions of poems and critical articles were an important part of the magazine and of his own literary development.

In 1943 Dudek and his wife, Stephanie, left for New York. Dudek intended to study journalism and history at Columbia University. Instead, a variety of influences led him to enter the master's program in English, for which he completed a thesis entitled "Thackeray and the Profession of Letters." During this same period, he was beginning to be recognized as a poet. His work was included in the Ryerson anthology *Unit of Five* (1944), edited by Ronald Hambleton; and in 1946 Ryerson published his first book, *East of the City*.

In 1951, after teaching English at the City College of New York and working on his Ph.D. dissertation, "The Relations between Literature and the Press," Dudek returned to Montreal to a teaching position at McGill. Although Dudek had continued to contribute to *First Statement* and its successor, *Northern Review*, he had become increasingly disaffected with Sutherland's conservatism and thus was attracted to a new magazine, *Contact*, edited by another *Unit of Five* alumnus, Raymond Souster.

The purpose of *Contact* is aptly defined by Frank Davey in *Louis Dudek & Raymond Souster*:

> *Contact* was, then, like *First Statement*, *Direction* and *Enterprise*, a definite expression of literary discontent. Both Souster and Dudek saw the few existing Canadian periodicals as inadequate both to their personal publication needs and to the hopes they had for the future direction of Canadian writing. While they reacted to this situation differently — Dudek by working behind the scenes, Souster by direct action — the message which they projected through *Contact* was clear: Canadian poetry magazines were conventional and parochial; Canadian writers were isolated and technically naïve; international writing was rapidly leaving a static Canadian literature behind.[5]

Souster's own comment shows just what form this direct action would take. His magazine would be "an outlet for experiment and a franker discussion of the directions poetry is to take, not articles on lampman [sic] and the movies."[6]

Dudek's involvement was, as Davey notes, primarily behind the scenes, but the vibrant character of *Contact* is in many ways representative of his own work in the period. The 1950s were Dudek's most prolific years as a poet. In 1952 his Ryerson chapbook *The Searching Image* was published, as well as *Cerberus* (with Irving Layton and Raymond Souster) and *Twenty-four Poems*, both by Contact Press, a new publishing venture started by Dudek, Layton, and Souster. In later years, Contact published the following books of poetry by Dudek: *Europe* (1954), *The Transparent Sea* (1956), *En México* (1958), and *Laughing Stalks* (1958).

Even with this outpouring, Dudek maintained other interests. In 1957 he began publishing his own magazine, *Delta*, which he continued, solely under his control, until 1966. As well, he created the McGill Poetry Series, first publisher of Leonard Cohen. In

1967, the year that Contact Press folded, Dudek began Delta Canada with the publication of his own *Atlantis*. Delta Canada subsequently published his *Collected Poetry* (1971) and the works of many others, including R.G. Everson and F.R. Scott, both under Delta Canada and its later imprint, DC Books.

Dudek has always been a critic as well as a poet, and since the 1960s the former occupation has perhaps overshadowed the latter. In 1960 *Literature and the Press: A History of Printing, Printed Media, and Their Relation to Literature*, a revision of his Ph.D. dissertation, was published, and in 1967 a series which he presented on CBC radio was printed as *The First Person in Literature*. The best reflection of Dudek's achievement as a critic is *Selected Essays and Criticism* (1978), a collection of forty-eight pieces from throughout his career. Even given this number, it is by no means complete. Particularly of note among the exclusions are the various cultural reactions he wrote for *The Gazette* [Montreal].

Until his retirement this year (1984), Dudek continued to lecture on modern poetry as Greenshields Professor of English at McGill University. Outside the university, he has spoken on the same subject to such audiences as the Canadian Council of Teachers of English and the Royal Society of Canada. A collection of these speeches has been published as *Technology and Culture* (1979).

For a period, Dudek's published poetry was primarily limited to occasional appearances in magazines. The exceptions were *Epigrams* (1975), a diffuse collection of very short pieces, and *Selected Poems* (1975). Lately, however, there has been a new flurry of activity, represented in *Cross-Section: Poems 1940–1980* (1980), a collection of previously unpublished short poems, *Poems from Atlantis* (1980), a reprint of passages from *Atlantis*, and a special edition of *Open Letter*, entitled *Louis Dudek: Texts & Essays* (1981), which is primarily a collection of Dudek's prose but also includes an interview and some drafts from *Europe*, *Atlantis*, and *Continuation I*. *Continuation I* (1981) is Dudek's latest long poem. He had previously published parts of it in *Collected Poetry* and in *The Tamarack Review* (Summer 1976).

LOUIS DUDEK

Tradition and Milieu

Though it may be difficult to ascertain objectively the tradition in which Louis Dudek should be placed, it is quite easy to see the continuum in which he would place himself. His criticism and his poetry have often been devoted to establishing a line which would define the development of modernism in poetry, in both an international and a Canadian context.

The influences behind Dudek's early poetry are seldom obvious. In his review of *Unit of Five*, after commenting on the English influences on the poetry of Ronald Hambleton, Northrop Frye stated, "Dudek on the other hand is a good poet who does not remind us of better ones...."[7] However, in an interview with John Nause and J. Michael Heenan, Dudek has noted at least one important connection for his early poetry:

> The Imagists were important to me personally from a very early time, even before I came in touch with the *First Statement* people, Layton and Sutherland. And these Imagists were Hilda Doolittle—H.D.—especially, and Richard Aldington....Imagism, for years, let's say for twenty years after this time of *First Statement*, was in all my teaching the central antidote to the ills of Canadian poetry: the insistence on clarity of imagery, contemporary imagery.[8]

Still, the influences which Dudek felt it most necessary to avoid were perhaps more important. These anti-influences were found in poetry which Dudek deemed to be aridly intellectual, formal, impersonal, and academic. The poets were usually British, particularly Eliot, Auden, and Spender. In "The Poetry of the Forties," Dudek's comments on the McGill poets suggest his reaction to those he sees as their forbears:

> Certainly the Scott-Smith generation did not move very far in the revolution of modern poetics. Klein never wrote a free-verse poem, so far as I know. Smith is an extremely traditionalist poet. Even Scott, the most modern of the three, follows the Auden reaction much of the time, with a return to metrics, a rational order of ideas, and lucid abstract exposition. Modernism, whatever it is, had a lot more than this to offer.[9]

There is an apparent contradiction here in that Dudek elsewhere is very much a proponent of "a rational order of ideas," and an admirer of Scott. The explanation is probably that Dudek feared a reductive ordering. As anyone who has read Dudek's poetry will attest, his method is always expansive.

Dudek and the others associated with *First Statement* often saw themselves in opposition to the contemporary little magazine *Preview*, edited by Patrick Anderson. In his interview with Nause and Heenan, Dudek calls Anderson a "visiting Britisher":

> And that's the crucial thing about it, that one magazine, *Preview*, was associated with what I think of, historically, as the colonial attachment of Canadian literature: their poetry had affinities with the English poetry of the preceding decade — especially Auden and Thomas — whereas the *First Statement* people were more related to contemporary American poetry, Twentieth-Century American poetry stemming out of Walt Whitman — Carl Sandburg, William Carlos Williams, and eventually Ezra Pound. (p. 31)

Central to Dudek at this time, as can be seen in his *First Statement* article "Academic Literature," was an overwhelming concern to avoid rarefied university verse:

> University writers may be good; but they are usually not much alive. There is usually a certain lack of liveliness, of the sense of reality, the human touch, a content of common sense. This is the difference between understanding through emotion and experience and through the book and the mind alone.[10]

Similarly, his early piece in *The McGill Daily*, "Whitman's Barbaric Yawp," emphasizes that part of Whitman which could not be contained by an academic view of literature: "Anybody who tries to analyse Walt's form will find that the problem is not a form but a man — you and me — as big as a universe — which cannot be reached by petty conniving reason."[11] Again this might seem an unlikely comment from the man whom Frank Davey, in *Louis Dudek & Raymond Souster*, repeatedly calls a "rationalist," but the distinction here is the qualifier, "petty conniving." The primary influence of Whitman on Dudek was this liberation, not from reason, but from the petty gentility that Dudek associated with the academic poets.

Still, Whitman's influence on Dudek has a number of other facets. Paul West has labelled Dudek as the most Whitmanesque among Canadian poets,[12] and Dudek himself has referred to Walt Whitman as "the father of us all."[13] In a comment Dudek made to Nause and Heenan about the ideas behind the *First Statement* group, Whitman surfaces once more: "I, too, was tremendously influenced by Nietzsche well before I met Layton. Not so much by Lawrence, but Nietzsche and Ibsen and Walt Whitman and Karl Marx. These were writers we read a great deal and talked about constantly" (p. 36). As well as the barbaric yawp, Whitman was a part of a philosophical ferment being explored by Dudek and his peers.

Thus, while Dudek felt anti-academic in many ways, he was by no means anti-intellectual. This might explain the apparent inconsistency of his entering Columbia University, where he was to meet a number of influential thinkers who were applying their talents to new analyses of European figures and events, in what is often called social history. Many of the ideas current at Columbia would not have been new to Dudek, but they were strongly reinforced by the arguments he heard. Jacques Barzun was developing his argument for a truly liberal education and for the importance of the intellectual élite, perhaps best summed up in his *The House of Intellect* (1959). Dudek presents a similar attitude in "F. R. Scott and the Modern Poets," in which he quotes Hannah Arendt's "The Mob and the Elite": ". . . only an inherent fundamental shortcoming of character in the intellectual, '*la trahison des clercs*' (J. Benda), or a perverse self-hatred of the spirit, accounted for the delight with which this élite accepted the 'ideas' of the mob."[14] Lionel Trilling touched on such subjects as the need for literature which traced the criticism of life, the quest for moral realism, the value of the study of the sociology of literature, and, perhaps most noteworthy, the importance of the little magazine.

During his first period at Columbia, Dudek was persuaded by the Canadian historian J. B. Brebner to read *A Revolution in European Poetry, 1660–1900* (1940) by Emery Neff. This was probably the most significant of the influences which Dudek assimilated at Columbia. Dudek's longest prose work, *Literature and the Press*, was dedicated to Neff, and many parts of it suggest the presence of his ideas. For instance, Dudek's portrayal of Carlyle as an embattled social critic is very similar to that found in Neff's *Carlyle* (1932). In fact, many of Dudek's quotations of Carlyle are taken from Neff's book. Neither Neff nor Dudek seems interested in the religious visionary of *Sartor Resartus*.

One factor common to Barzun, Trilling, and Neff is the importance of the great moral idea. The thought of a literature controlled by form rather than ideas, or of a literature without compelling moral purpose, was unacceptable to them. It might seem that Dudek's stated commitment to Imagism would have left him in conflict with these philosophies, for Dudek himself has noted how the Imagists "rejected ideas."[15] Still, throughout his work, in prose and poetry, Dudek has maintained that the appropriate poetic method is only a vehicle for the statement of the writer. Dudek has taken what amounts to a moral stance on the importance of the idea as presented by a committed individual. From this position, he has engaged in debate with opposing forces with a vigour which has at times approached verbal warfare.

The prime example must be one of his most unpopular causes, his defence of Ezra Pound as just such a committed writer. Pound must have seemed an appropriate reconciliation of the split between the image and the idea. The poet whom Dudek quotes as saying "Go in fear of abstractions"[16] became one of the most ideology-laden writers of the twentieth century. Dudek has said,

> Pound meant a lot to me, but not to anyone else. That is, amongst the people I move around with, nobody was very much influenced or much concerned with Ezra Pound. Not Layton, not Souster, not Earle Birney. What he was for me, I would say, was a kind of synthesis or focus for all the problems that I saw in poetry, beginning with the aesthetic position, the notion of art in poetry.[17]

His personal relationship with Pound began with a letter in 1949, followed by a vigorous correspondence until 1953 and periodic letters after that. Dudek preserved Pound's letters and published them in 1974, together with an account of one visit to

Pound and the transcript of a radio program he did on Pound, as *Dk/Some Letters of Ezra Pound.* In many ways a curious book, *Dk* reproduces the letters in the original type with notes by Dudek which combine detailed scholarly annotation and very personal reactions. Dudek makes clear his evaluation of Pound: "Ezra Pound is the most important single force in the shaping of modern poetry."[18] "He was a very great poet. The greatest in our time" (*Dk*, p. 143). Yet he also recognizes, in a number of comments, the necessity of explaining that his support for Pound was not without limitations:

> I was very much in agreement with Pound's general motives and significance — his principles of action — but I was also very clear in my own mind about the narrow specific program which he was determined to impose on his followers: I found this dogmatic program repugnant and absurd. From this point in the correspondence, the ambiguity of my devotion to Pound — a devotion which continues to this day — and the pattern of my resistance to him become increasingly clear. I believe that his narrow dogmatism was a product of his mental illness; but this illness, though devastating and tragic for him, did not penetrate very deep, it was a surface mania. Behind it, within it, surrounding it, was the brilliant and generous intelligence with which I wanted to communicate. It was this intelligence that was afflicted with a mania, like a great gothic window smashed and lying in fragments on the cathedral floor, but still keeping its magnificent design intact. (*Dk*, p. 90)

The discursive nature of Dudek's major poems, *Europe*, *En México*, and *Atlantis*, shows a clear influence from Pound's *Cantos*; as well, the manner in which Dudek presents his observations reflects a number of Pound's poetic theories, most obviously the ideogram, the creation of a poetic version of the Chinese visual representation of an idea (*FPL*, p. 58). But there is a severe limit to Dudek's acceptance of Pound's economic and social theories. One area of disagreement can be detected between Dudek's nationalism and Pound's internationalism. Pound reacts to Dudek's devotion to the local literary scene with:

"naturally to HELL with Canadian or any other parrochial [sic] pt / of view" (*Dk.* p. 88). But Dudek chose to remain very much within the Canadian literary world, even though one might see some second thoughts in a number of his comments in *Epigrams*: "We have a completely new Canadian literature every twenty years. It just doesn't stand up any longer than that." "The main handicap of the Canadian writer is that he has to write for Canadians."[19]

Dudek does not seem to have been directly influenced very much by Canadian writers. He has expressed esteem for a number of older Canadians, including Archibald Lampman, E. J. Pratt, and F. R. Scott,[20] but one is hard-pressed to find much evidence of their examples in Dudek's work. Concerning his contemporaries, their support (or nonsupport) is less central to his poetry than to his career as a poet, and in this latter regard, his relationship with Irving Layton was probably most important. A. J. M. Smith once described it as follows:

> Layton shall how to flatter Layton teach,
> And modest Dudek Dudek's glories preach;
> *Layton* shall tingle in Canadian air,
> And echo answer *Dudek* everywhere.[21]

In fact, their relationship was never so absolute. Dudek's acclaim for the early Layton was strong and yet measured. Of *First Statement*, he said to Wynne Francis, "I always felt myself 'third.' Sutherland was the leader and editor, Layton was 'the poet'—we all expected he would soon be recognized — and I was best at handling the mechanics of the printing press" (p. 8).

Dudek and Layton seem to have shared a philosophical position at this time but it is difficult to define what it was, other than vaguely left-wing and anti-establishment. In their prefaces to *Cerberus*, both Dudek and Layton called for freedom, love, and intelligence, and for an opposition to gentility. Dudek stated, "We three in this book share the same affirmations and therefore the same negations in the face of the present."[22] Nonetheless, even at this point, there were clearly varying responses. Dudek asserted a need for order: ". . . it is imagination—as poetry, faith, ethics — which gives order and beauty to life" (p. 13). Layton declared: ". . . the best part of any man today is the hell he carries inside him..." (p.45). They both rejected the restraint of earlier poetry, but Dudek saw the restraint replaced by a new higher order. Layton returned to one of Dudek's themes, Whitman's "yawp," but used it in support of, not a new order, but an anarchic destructive confrontation: "Whitman's 'barbaric yawp' is wanted to send them finger-plugging their ears and scurrying for cover under their tea-tables" (p.46).

When Layton began to be generally recognized by critics, Dudek reacted in 1956 with "Layton Now and Then," in which he attacked a review by A.J.M. Smith published earlier that year.[23] Dudek's primary point of confrontation is that Smith had presented a very inadequate view of Layton in dismissing his early poems. Dudek's own opinion is not stated directly, but he leaves the impression that he now felt closer to the early Layton than the later. From this, it was only a short time until his direct rejection of the new work. In 1958 Dudek referred to "Layton's recent well-nigh demented poetry."[24] It would seem that in Dudek's opinion Layton's exploration of "the hell he carries inside him" had gone too far. A year later, in "Layton on the Carpet," Dudek wrote, "I must confess that for the past three or four years I've been unable to read anything by Irving Layton, at any rate not without a certain feeling of sour taste and acid indigestion."[25] Layton's reaction was a typically Laytonic open letter to Dudek:

> When a poet dies there's a special smell that ascends to heaven; for twenty-four hours no ant shits. Piss, brine and toadeye are useless. Now as you pass, professors pick their noses less thoughtfully, female poets regard their crotches hopelessly, and virginal queens command the instant destruction of all barber poles.[26]

Dudek's relationships with other poets have been less tempestuous, but also perhaps less important. An exception might be his connection with Raymond Souster, though once again it seems a question of mutual support and publishing cooperation, rather than stylistic influence. Dudek's effect on the younger generation of poets is even less clear. There have been a number of little magazines directly or indirectly shaped by his influence. *CIV/n* and *Yes* were edited by his protégés, Aileen Collins and Michael

Gnarowski, respectively. *It Needs to Be Said* was similarly in Dudek's footsteps, as noted in the editorial to its Louis Dudek issue (No. 4 [1974]). Dudek has also given editorial and even financial support to a number of young poets. Still, it is difficult to see much connection between his own poetry and that of the younger generation, though one of these younger writers, Frank Davey, makes the opposite judgement:

> Louis Dudek has had the most influence on subsequent generations of Canadian poetry of any poet in Canadian literary history. His lyrics, that build from anecdote or observation to a punchline of humour or philosophy, have provided one of the commonest structures in recent Canadian verse, being evident in the work of Al Purdy, George Bowering, Seymour Mayne, Michael Ondaatje, Lionel Kearns, Alden Nowlan, John Newlove, to name only a few. His work with the structure of the long meditational poem has marked the beginning of a period in which widespread experiment in this form has been one of the unique characteristics of Canadian poetry. Notable among those following Dudek's lead here, although usually without his didacticism, have been Bowering, Victor Coleman, Daphne Marlatt, Frank Davey, bpNichol, and Dennis Lee.[27]

I would still tend to see most of these forms as extending back to a similar, usually American, source, but Davey's experience as poet, editor, and critic makes his analysis worthy of consideration.

Critical Overview and Context

There are a variety of opinions on Louis Dudek, but few have been found in print. In conversation, most Canadian poets and critics will make a judgement, but only Frank Davey has produced a book on Dudek, and even Davey splits his volume between Dudek and Raymond Souster. There have been only three major articles published — all in *Canadian Literature*. Even the reviews are slim. His early books received the same two or three notices one would expect for a new poet, but his later works have seldom done much better.

Northrop Frye's early praise of Dudek's contribution to *Unit of Five* was noted above. He suggested a real possibility of later achievement: "Dudek's poetry, I hope, looks to the immediate future, to a wider and sounder appreciation of poetry, and to a corresponding increase of the poet's self-confidence."[28] B.K. Sandwell's reaction to the same book was quite different: "How angry Mr. Louis Dudek is I do not know, for I cannot profess to understand most of him, and what I do understand seems hardly worth understanding."[29]

E.K. Brown had found this selection of Dudek's work to lack any "core of unity,"[30] and when he came to Dudek's own book, *East of the City*, he reflected, "Perhaps what one misses most is what Mr. Finch has in such perfection, the distinctive power over words, the individual word, and the arrangement of words in broad units."[31] A.J.M. Smith also found himself comparing Dudek with Robert Finch, but without slighting one for the other: "It is a quality of *manliness*, as contrasted with Mr. Finch's *gentlemanliness*, which distinguishes the latest and best of Mr. Dudek's poems...."[32]

It would seem that Smith here is touching on the distinction which Dudek himself would have made between his own work and Finch's. At the same time, Earle Birney saw in *East of the City* some of the qualities that Dudek had just attacked in his *First Statement* article, "Academic Literature." Quoting from that article, Birney singled out " 'a preference for word-patterns rather than poetry' and 'for the unnatural exploitation of the vivid image' "; yet he also saw a quality in Dudek which the latter would have esteemed: "Dudek has that rare gift of the true poet, the ability to savor the most ordinary experience with the freshness of a child and to write about it with the subtlety of an adult."[33]

In reference to *Cerberus*, Frye continued his praise of Dudek, elevating him well above the other contributors, Souster and Layton. Frye's assessment of the development of Dudek might say more about Frye's prejudices than about Dudek's poetry, but it is of interest in light of Dudek's later work:

> In deference to his colleagues, Mr. Dudek endeavours to recapture some of his earlier feeling for social problems, but it is clear from his manifesto that he is no longer in danger of confusing poetry with popular rhetoric. He realizes that

> the enemy of poetry is not social evil but slipshod language, the weasel words that betray the free mind: he realizes that to create requires an objective serenity beyond all intruding moral worries about atomic bombs and race prejudice.[34]

Europe immediately presented itself as something worthy of note. Margaret Heideman stated, "A poem so large in scope and intent is a signal event in Canadian poetry."[35] But by the end of her review, she suggested that the various flaws in the work make it at best an ambivalent pleasure. Milton Wilson had a similar mixed feeling, although he began with the negative: "At first, as the long line of platitudes started to file past in limp, undistinguished verse, I was frankly incredulous. I had not supposed that Mr. Dudek, whose talent I respect, could be so unabashedly dull."[36]

The discursive nature of the poem led many to note the scent of Ezra Pound, usually seen to be harmful. Mona Van Duyn, in *Poetry* [Chicago], observed, "One might have been warned by familiar references to 'Ezra' earlier in the book, I suppose."[37] The clearest presentation of this position again came from Northrop Frye:

> The century of meditation is a fatal idea for a facile poet, and although at his best Mr. Dudek escapes being merely facile, I find large stretches of the book unrewarding. In the first place, the influence of Pound is oppressive. Pound is everywhere: the rub-a-dub three- and four-accent line, the trick of snapped-up quotations and allusions, the harangues against usura, the tobaggan-slide theory of the decline of Europe after the Middle Ages, and so on. In the second place, the conversational style brings the ideas into sharp relief, and the ideas are commonplace, prejudice reinforced by superficial tourism.[38]

Wilson, on the other hand, suggested that Pound's presence is not all to the bad: "... in a cathedral or the Wordsworth country, he has eyes and convictions, and the influence of Ezra Pound, so deadly when Mr. Dudek is not operating at high efficiency, is now life-giving."[39]

When *The Transparent Sea*, a selected poems, appeared,

Kildare Dobbs attacked directly: "Most of his work is forced or insipid; but posterity will remember him as the man who played Billy Graham to Irving Layton's Messiah."[40] A more reasoned and probably more accurate judgement came from Chester Duncan:

> One is often so grateful for Mr. Dudek's prolificacy and so fearful of the narrow donnish strictness that he avoids that one wants to take it all and damn the analysts. Yet in the future it's going to be difficult to prove that he is a good poet except in his capacity as phrasemaker.[41]

Laughing Stalks, a collection of satires, and *En México* came out at much the same time, and so were often reviewed together. The general reaction seems to have been to praise *En México*, with limitations, and to reject *Laughing Stalks*. Desmond Pacey, however, reversed the process with the following comment on *En México*: "This is much the weaker of the two books — a kind of meditative travelogue à la *Europe*. Platitudes are dressed up to masquerade as wisdom, but the disguise is usually only too transparent."[42] Frye was not wholeheartedly won by Dudek's version of the long poem, but he judged *En México* to be a major improvement over *Europe*: "In this poem Mr. Dudek has matured his technique of indented lines and parenthetical rhythms, and the gentle rocking sway of this meditative poem is full of a contemplative charm."[43] Yet Al Purdy seems to have grasped the ambivalence that governs critics of Dudek's verses in a very personal reaction to *Laughing Stalks* and *En México*: "These are capsule, chile con carne philosophy and observation, good or bad depending on your perspective to Popocatepetl or Montreal. They are not trivial, downright bad, to be dismissed lightly. (A good poet wrote them.) But they're not my dish."[44]

By the publication of *Atlantis* in 1967, the ambivalent critic had become *de rigueur.* Len Gasparini suggested something different: "Louis Dudek's book-length quasi-epic might be unopprobriously labelled 'The Great Late Un-Canadian Poem,' or 'The Wanderjahr of a Middle-Class Canadian Poet in the Old World.' "[45] His final judgement, however, was not dissimilar from the norm, perhaps best represented by Peter Stevens: "*Atlantis* is an uneven poem, filled with sections of sweep and movement, pulled down by rather prosaic, meandering and haphazard intellectualization."[46]

Besides individual reviews, there have been three major articles written on Dudek's work. "A Critic of Life: Louis Dudek as Man of Letters," by Wynne Francis, has been quoted from already. It is essentially biographical, a description of Dudek's career as a man of letters, with "a secure place in the history of modern Canadian literature" (p. 23). Douglas Barbour, in "Poet as Philosopher," emphasizes Dudek's attempt to present a reasoned essay in poetry, something quite different from the poet as "incredible madman":

> Pound was just such a madman, but Dudek pleases us most when he is rational, meditative, the philosopher to be listened to and argued with, but not possessed by.
>
> We are overburdened these days with "possessed" and "incredible" madmen in poetry. But there is no one else to speak to us in the reasonable, honourable, voice of intellectual integrity that is Louis Dudek's. Too many younger writers have been ignorant of his work and the possibilities for poetry that it represents.[47]

Francis and Barbour are informative, but they provide few of the novel insights which Dorothy Livesay provides in "The Sculpture of Poetry." This entire essay is of value, but some brief references can suggest Livesay's position. She asserts that Dudek's early work is "concerned not with sound effects so much as with pictures in rhythmic arrangement."[48] She continues by maintaining that his later works, apparently so prosaic, have a similar base: "Quite frequently the poems seem to lack drama and dramatic tension, but they are a true rhythmic mirror of the poet's intention. No word or phrase can be taken away; none can be added" (p. 31). By careful and detailed analysis of the stress and all aspects of sound, she decides, "Sound harmonies then, together with a beautifully balanced phrasal pattern, enhance the *conceptual* conclusion which is the theme of all Louis Dudek's poetry: that harmony and order in nature towards which mankind strives" (p. 35). In her estimation, Dudek is "the contemporary Canadian poet most consciously concerned with shape, form and sound: the origins of rhythm" (p. 26).

During 1980–81 Frank Davey single-handedly did much to increase awareness of Dudek's work. Davey's belief in Dudek's influence on Canadian poetry has already been noted in a quotation from *From There to Here*. Davey's special issue of *Open Letter*, *Louis Dudek: Texts & Essays*, begins with a still more polemical statement:

> Through this collection we believe Dudek's centrality to Canadian poetry will become indisputably apparent. His work binds Smith, Scott, and Klein to the writing of the present generation. It links Canadian writing to the great modernist descent from Joyce, Pound, Eliot, and Williams. It holds McLuhan's examination of mid-twentieth-century technology tightly to the context of the modernist struggle to achieve value and meaning despite the overwhelming dedication to commodity of the culture at large. Dudek is a successor to Pound, standing unshadowed in the company of Bunting, Olson, and Spicer. His long poems, the first major modernist poems in Canadian literature, open up formal possibilities which are later to dominate important work by Marlatt, Bowering, Nichol, Lee, and Kroetsch. As Wynne Francis has noted, Dudek is also the first "man of letters" in Canada, the first to follow Arnold and Pound in combining poetry, criticism, polemic editing, and cultural criticism into one multi-faceted cultural vision.[49]

Davey's major statement to date on Dudek is his book *Louis Dudek & Raymond Souster* (1980). As one might expect from Davey's other comments, he is most at home when examining Dudek's longer poems, but at times he seems so much at home he becomes Dudek's apologist. In discussing how the form of Dudek's poetry responds to poetic intent, he asserts,

> Dudek would probably consider *Atlantis* a near perfect poem. The poem corresponds almost exactly to the aesthetic and moral theories it propounds. The few very moving passages in which Dudek exerts the full range of his artistic power to display a passionately perceived situation are confined to those relatively infrequent moments when "paradise" reveals itself.... Until the very end, most of the

> poetry in *Atlantis* is desultory and unremarkable, like the world the poet perceives. When Dudek finds only trivia and boredom, which happens most of the time, he responds faithfully to the experience and resists all temptation to "dress" it up with rhyme and rhetoric. (pp. 76–77)

This would seem quite in tune with Dudek's latest attempts in *Continuation 1* to produce a long poem which is a casual accounting of the poet's experiences. Still, Davey's argument seems like a cunning justification of banal verse: boring poetry is acceptable if its purpose is to depict boredom.

On the other hand, Davey's analysis of *Europe* succeeds in elucidating a method which may be apparent to most readers but usually seems unexplainable:

> Although arranged chronologically, its ninety-nine sections in no sense form a narrative; the *story* of Dudek's travels is not the subject of the poem. The poet's reactions are continuous with the poem's aesthetic premises; Dudek consistently recoils from sham, hypocrisy, avarice and self-importance but warms to honesty and authenticity. *Europe* thus has a wholeness, an integrity of vision in which language and form obey the same moral view that informs the poet's opinions and judgements. (p. 54)

This comment on the link between language, form, and a moral vision is very close to what Davey identifies as Dudek's general philosophy:

> Aesthetics are an extension of moral vision. This belief, which has been a prerequisite to most of the great art of the world, is seldom respected in Canada where writers have usually struggled to achieve competence rather than greatness. Thus Dudek's work has not been intelligently or sympathetically received. Yet his work is courageous precisely because it sacrifices popularity in order to strive for something remarkable. (p. 81)

The other central tenets identified by Davey and linked to this moral vision are Dudek's rationalism and modernism. Davey asserts that as Dudek developed, he turned from a dependence on Imagism, what Davey refers to as "the perceptual process" (p. 50), to a devotion to thought, which Davey presents as "the reasoning process" (p. 50). Later in the book, Davey states, "Dudek's first criterion, 'the ability to think,' relates to the rationalist bias that pervades all his poetry and criticism except *Literature and the Press*" (p. 89).

Davey's reference to "all" Dudek's poetry seems to contradict his claim that Dudek's concern moved from the image to the idea. It has already been noted, however, that Dudek was devoted to both idea and image, regardless of the conflict between perception and reason. Davey himself provides a partial explanation in his synopsis of Dudek's personal form of modernism:

> Throughout his mature work Dudek has espoused an evolved modernism which seeks a transcendental vision expressed in temporal form and idiom and rooted in the here and now. He makes his primary commitment to historical time and cultural realities. His modernism is humanist in its attachment to contemporary life but antihumanist in its belief in transcendent vision as the ultimate artistic goal. (p. 162)

Dudek's attention is on things humanistic. His basic method is formed out of Imagism. But the result which he seeks from this attention and method is transcendent. Dudek himself presents the most clear working out of these conflicts in "The Theory of the Image in Modern Poetry," in which he concludes, "A poem, of course, is partly about experience and existence as we know it. But its greatest power, if it is a true poem, derives from the faint hint or suggestion it gives of that other, unknown world of being."[50]

Davey's careful analysis will probably do much to increase interest in Dudek's work, but it seems likely that Dudek will maintain his ambiguous position on the Canadian poetic ladder. For those interested in quantification, the *Supplement to the Oxford Companion to Canadian History and Literature* (1973) gives him 115 lines. This places him ahead of Souster, Scott, and Purdy but behind Layton, Reaney, and Birney. His *Collected Poetry* was termed by John Robert Colombo to be "the best —

and most overlooked—book to appear in the last decade."[51] Mel Dagg equivocated slightly before asserting that "...this collection reveals him to be one of Canada's finest poets."[52] But, for the most part, the ambivalence continues; as Michael Hornyansky observed:

> Still, for all my skepticism about building visions from incremental fragments, I'm fascinated enough to revisit. Is it because of the ideas and hints so richly poured forth, showering sparks and echoes, a warehouse of material for a make-it-yourself poem; or is it because of the immense energy of the man, surging and pounding away (with credits to Ezra) at the untamable universe?[53]

Dudek's Works

The lack of agreement among various critics of Dudek's work reflects the often amorphous nature of that work. Regardless of the cohesion described by Livesay in "The Sculpture of Poetry," and suggested by the title of Karol Wenek's unpublished M.A. thesis, "Louis Dudek's Acropolis of Words: Towards the New Democratic Age," Dudek's poetry, being too concerned with the needs of the new age, at times lacks even a minimal attention to the sculpting of his acropolis. In the longer poems, Dudek's philosophic observations sometimes appear to be presented in an arbitrary manner. The usual critical reaction has been to note some good elements but to reject the works as wholes. Dudek's recent publication of *Poems from Atlantis* suggests that even he now feels compelled to respond to this fragmentary appreciation.

The ambivalence of Dudek's audience is at least partly a reflection of various choices he has made in his development as a poet and a critic. Surprisingly, these choices are seldom related to his general philosophical position, for his ideological stance was established early and has varied only slightly. The important changes in his poetry have been formal ones, from the lyric to the long meditation and lately to the epigram.

The changes in his criticism have been not so much internal as external. They have been reactions to perceived changes in the poets and literary world around him. Thus, the conflict with

Irving Layton, which no doubt has a strong personal component, could also be explained by the difference between Layton's contemporary poetry and that of what Dudek sees as the old "vigorous realistic poet."[54] In general, Dudek's prime characteristic as a critic has been the disinterestedness so often called for by Matthew Arnold. Dudek has behaved according to the dictum which should be followed by all critics, but often is not: literature is too important for the critic to be swayed by friendship or by a personal enmity.

From the beginning of his career, Dudek has asserted the importance of literature, and particularly of poetry, as a potential influence on society. The group at *The McGill Daily* felt this to be a central concern of the age. A pseudonymous columnist, "Cryptic," wrote the following about "real artists":

> They are social artists, people who live in this world and have a responsibility. They are not mystical "individualists" but true individuals who fully find themselves in the concretization of the demands of the people for a better life.... They have something of vital importance to say to people.[55]

Reference has already been made to Dudek's own early article "Whitman's Barbaric Yawp," which appeared in *The McGill Daily* in 1940. A still more revealing piece is "Soliloquy of an Amoeba," published in the same paper in 1938. The speaker questions man's supremacy: "Now I see the development of the amoeba as a gradual and progressive change from the lowest form of life, which is man, to the highest, that which gives the greatest efficiency with the minimum of effort." The amoeba points out that he is able to fulfil the requirements of being an amoeba perfectly, whereas the human is quite unsuccessful at his role. The amoeba notes that man's intelligence causes "crazy delusions, vanities, errors of ignorance and judgement, all of which constitute a horrible chaos known as human society."[56]

Superficially, this article might be seen as simply an attack by an unbiased observer, an amoeba, on the vices of our modern society. Beneath this, however, there is an ironic comment on contemporary man's concern for order. If our aim is simply to increase efficiency, the best bet is to emulate the bland, useless life of the amoeba. In later works, Dudek has suggested that modern technology might be leading us to this amoebalike mediocrity. Complete efficiency leaves no room for the freedom to take individual, human, approaches to life.

"Soliloquy" is quite similar in style to Dudek's later prose. He has increased the fluidity of his language, but he has maintained the polemical, highly rhetorical delivery. From the very start, Dudek was not attracted to the careful restraint which marks a Northrop Frye or Frank Davey, even when their content is most radical.

Dudek's early poetry is arguably much less of a piece with his later work. The selections in *Unit of Five* demonstrate the clear influence, usually positive, of the Imagists. "Improvisation," which Dudek later selected to begin his *Collected Poetry*, begins with precise images, examined from a precise physical stance. This is the form of much early Dudek, comparable perhaps to the wandering eavesdropper found so often in Souster.

"Improvisation" moves, however, from this simple conversational observation to something akin to a Canadian Whitman:

> I rise in elevators where the derricks run
> and trail on the prairies,
> seeing grain stores stand like thirsting men;
> machinery on Charlie Chaplin feet
> speeds, and sticks, and comes to a halt
> and speeds again.

The poem concludes with a vision which again owes much to Whitman:

> Like electricity that darts and ceases,
> my eyes filling my eyelids
> trace a face seen only on misted mornings
> or in vertigoes of star-swept skies;
> and in the midst of these, secret as any,
> they move and move in the quick atmosphere.[57]

Within the limits of his conversational form, Dudek shows a consciously poetic approach. The limited use of adverbs and adjectives and the concentration on physical images, even when presenting a thought which does not lend itself to such a presentation, show how Dudek had learned Pound's "Go in fear of abstractions."[58] The chice of words might be even too poetic in sound: "trace a face," "misted mornings," and "star-swept skies."

The overtly political poetry of this period shows a very different side of Dudek, in a rhetoric which the Imagists would not have been likely to countenance. In "A Factory on Sunday," he refers to the chimney as "a tower built for a strange god":

> But it is also the bossed bludgeon
> Of the ape-man and barbarian:
> A symbol of his lust for power
> Set in the ground to stand
> In the sight of the cowed and beaten.
>
> (*CP*, p.5)

At this stage in his career, Dudek was still willing, at times, to write in response to a felt political duty, rather than following his critical call for the individual thinker or his poetic search for image and form.

In *Unit of Five*, one poem, "The Sea," gives clear suggestions of Dudek's later work. He is still limiting himself to precise images, without the tendency to diffusion which would appear later. The two- and three-stress lines are much shorter than he came to employ, and the tight four-line stanzas and conventional rhymes similarly suggest the early Dudek. Nonetheless, the cumulative effect is like that of his later meditations, and the use of the sea as a catalyst to reflection will come to dominate *Europe* and *Atlantis*. "The Sea" concludes:

> Till barebacked, whole, and hard,
> Rending the deep,
> Leviathan continents shall rise
> Where oceans sleep,
>
> And portals your lime and clay
> Shall open apart,
> In cities high with wonder
> Of heroic art...

O for these, the cities,
(Hear the wind!)
Shall the fire of your bones
Be cold, be stilled.

(*CP*, p. 9)

The apocalyptic vision, the hope for a heroic art of a new civilization, and the central symbol of Atlantis all herald Dudek's later works.

Dudek's critical articles of the same period show the beginnings of his search for the ideal literature, the focus of almost all of his prose. In "Poets of Revolt...or Reaction?" he notes, "Today, a revolution is being accomplished, in which all white shirts are soiled. The *sabotniki* are out. Poets are dragged into the streets with the rest...."[59] Dudek's politics press him to praise this dragging. He observes one poet who seemed to become one with the common man, Carl Sandburg, but Dudek recognizes him to be "almost unique." Sandburg is contrasted with the majority of social reformers who write poems which tend to be "comic satirical" and "intellectual" and thereby detach the poet from the people. It is worthy of note that Dudek includes one of his own works in this category.

The first piece chosen by Michael Gnarowski[60] for Dudek's *Selected Essays and Criticism* is "Academic Literature," mentioned above. As Earle Birney pointed out, a number of the faults which Dudek presents in this article are found in Dudek's own poetry. Perhaps more important, Dudek was rejecting the university as an appropriate habitation for a poet two years before he would return to what has proved to be a lifelong association with academe. Nevertheless, when most ideological, Dudek's poetry has been tied to specific personal experience, as in his meditations on travel, and his academic life has never broken that concern for reality. Yet it has contributed to the very heavy presence of "the book and the mind,"[61] the dominance of which he saw as such a danger in "Academic Literature."

In *East of the City*, Dudek had his first opportunity to present his own book of poetry. Once again the influence of Imagism is strong, but still stronger is the liberated individual, the visionary all-seeing "I":

I am walking full of poems; I make them
hitting home runs, taking the sun,
worrying, looking at people.
I am breathing under the excitement.
("Making Poems," in *CP*, p. 13)

"Making Poems" begins the volume. At the conclusion of the book, he comes back to the same subject in "On Poetry": "this is poetry, action unrealized: / what we want most we imagine most, like self-abusing boys" (*CP*, p. 24). Dudek suggests that "...the poet, who had vision, / wanted to be capable of commanding God, like Jeremiah; / but denied, he ranted poetry" (*CP*, p. 24). Dudek sees the failure of the poet, but he retains an admiration for his romantic vision.

"On Poetry" also demonstrates the beginning of Dudek's direct use of another stage of Pound's theories. Regardless of Pound's earlier statements about abstractions, he came, particularly in the *Cantos*, to extend his ideogrammic method to the point where an abstract idea became the image. In the conversational tone of "On Poetry," in what might be Barbour's voice of reason,[62] Dudek is slowly moving in a similar direction.

At this point, however, the motion is still tentative. The poems continue to emphasize the physical image as recorded by the wandering poet-observer. *East of the City* includes some of Dudek's last works in this form which present an overtly left-wing message. They are also his best propagandist pieces. In the title poem, Dudek shows how adept he was at "socialist realism," the bold outline of the evils of capitalism and the courage of the workers:

They sling their thumbs through their lax suspenders
On rags of shirt crossing their barren shoulders,
Wipe the wrinkles round their throats and ear-lobes,
And plod the streets together....
(*CP*, p. 33)

I think the success of such poems is in these portraits, but the pictures are at times overwhelmed by the polemic, as in "Building a Skyscraper":

And then, a colosseum will be made of the street,
sidewalks will become benches, and windows break with
cheers.
We will praise "Men Working." They will be celebrated
more than millionaires, since without rich men
nations can run as well, or better, but not without these men.
And because they now work inaudibly, cursing behind a
fence,
I know that someday, over the applause and clamour
of the crowd, will fall on every ear the workman's hammer.
(*CP*, p. 45)

The mention of "socialist realism" suggests the controversy that arose some thirty years later between Dudek and Dorothy Livesay, another poet who has been known to write similarly propagandist phrases. The little magazine *It Needs to Be Said* had dedicated its fourth issue to Dudek and to the support of "social realism." The fifth issue included a letter from Livesay in response. She noted Dudek's early socialist poetry but gave the following assessment of his present stance: "... the man is a reactionary individualist and in no way a bearer of the torch for struggle and change through social realism."[63] In the next number, Dudek gave his own in return, calling Livesay a "push-button leftist," but he also went on to clarify his own view of his social realism:

Political concern, or social concern, does not necessarily mean conformity to the pigeon-holes of the 1930's. There can be social concern, and realism, outside the mild fanaticisms of "right" and "left." Also, the "social values" for which one is concerned can be much larger than merely those of property and so-called class interest. If my life-savings are smaller than they should be (and they are!) because I have put my money into publishing poetry instead of into business, that makes me a humanitarian and a politically-active poet as much as if I had contributed my money to charities and to labour unions.

Therefore building civilization is a social and political activity—though Dorothy will probably not agree.[64]

Thus Dudek sees himself as a continuous "social realist." Although his definition of this stance is very loose, it appears to reject the limitations implied in "socialist realism," which Dudek presumably would now see as one of the "mild fanaticisms."

During the 1950s, Dudek gradually defined this position in both prose and poetry. In his article "F.R. Scott and the Modern Poets" (1950), much of his assessment is suggestive of self-analysis:

> It is as if Canada were not yet ready to allow a first-rate mind to devote itself wholly to poetry. In F.R. Scott, the moral energy, the active part of the "faith" which he had inherited, was turned to the work of social analysis and political reconstruction. As a leader in the CCF Party he attempted to write the poem of political reality which Edmund Wilson once predicted would someday replace poetry entirely; and this could only be done at the expense of the poem of imagination on the printed page.[65]

Dudek seems to lament the tendency to choose the political road to change, rather than the poetical.

In "Où sont les jeunes?" (1952), in the first issue of *Contact*, he makes an assessment of the poetical road which shows how close he remained to Pound and Imagism:

> Let there be concrete images: let them grow into symbols, drama, physical experiments, nightmares or apocalyptic fantasies; but let the poem be made of pigs and perambulators, not — ness, — tion, — uth![66]

Dudek's contemporary poetry often holds to this line, but again his elevated sensibility often brings him very close to the abstract. One of his most popular poems from this period, "The Pomegranate," from *The Searching Image*, concentrates on the physical but concludes in the following manner:

> And can this fact be made, so big, of the body, then?
> And is beauty bounded all in its impatient mesh?
> The movement of the stars is that, and all their light
> Secretly bathed the world, that now flows out of flesh.
>
> (*CP*, p. 47)

In the same year, *Twenty-four Poems* demonstrates a more absolute devotion to concrete images, as in "A Small Rain," given here in its entirety:

Evening. With the thin rain falling.
A sky like moonstone.
And here, a slender tree, at street-edge
            one branch pointing left
                        skyward,
            another, thin, slanting to the right.
And in the pale-light-filled street
                    the first lamps, far
            pearly, light blue
                    light green, red
            of all colors
                    of all dimensions.[67]

Regardless of Dudek's stated views, however, when he came to collect his poetry twenty years later, he included only four works from this volume, none of them among the most obviously imagistic.

"A Small Rain" is one of Dudek's earlier experiments with spreading out his lines on the page. Another poem, "Line and Form," from *The Searching Image*, has a similar open structure but utilizes it in a discussion of its purpose:

Eternal forms.
The single power, working alone
        rounds out a parabola
                that flies into the infinite;
but the deflected particle
            out of that line, will fetch a frisk
                    of sixes and eights
                        before it vanishes:

an ocean arrested
            by sudden solid
                ripples out in the sand.

So this world of forms, having no scope for eternity,
                is created

in the limitation of what would be complete and
perfect,
achieving virtue only
by the justness of its compromises.
(*CP*, pp. 64–65)

Dudek here approaches the abstract intellectual argument which has been such a major part of his work. He suggests the necessity of finding the compromise form in which to represent that which can have no form. Once again, the ocean is an appropriate metaphor; he attempts to stop it for a moment as it reaches the mundane shore.

It would appear that the best term for Dudek's method here would be what Charles Olson defined as "composition by field," the arrangement of lines in accord with the different "fields" of idea and emotion, of subject and object. Still, Dudek's assessment of Olson's *In Cold Hell, in Thicket* and *The Maximus Poems* does not seem very positive:

> My own feeling, after both books, is that Olson should chuck all this self-analytical sentimental "buzzing" (Composition by Field or whatever theory) and get down to the old humble job of constructing a poem.[68]

Dudek provides another reaction to Olson in a poem from *Laughing Stalks*. In "To William Carlos Williams," he confronts Olson's belief that the line should follow the breath:

All right, all right, per cuss-
ive, Pro-
jec-
tive Verse if you please...
But then,
what if I don't like
the way he BREATHES?[69]

Dudek appears to be alienated by Olson's various theories, but he does not delineate the distinction from his own. One is tempted to see the major difference as simply a more conservative approach to similar methods. The best discussion which Dudek has given of form is in his "A Note on Metrics" (1958), published in *Delta*. A number of poets within and without Canada have noted this as a compelling argument:

> The inner ear, in all poetry since 1650, appreciates a more subtle, at any rate a different music from the noise made by the vocal chords. The poem it hears is the ideal sound, most private and personal; whereas the recited poem is always rough-handled and "interpreted" by another's voice and personality.[70]

He finds the most successful fruition of this in Williams, H.D., Wallace Stevens, E.E. Cummings, and, especially, Pound. He asserts, "Metre makes it easy to counterfeit poetry; with the new method each poem is an original piece of music, a form that cannot be borrowed or counterfeited."[71]

In *Delta*, in 1959, Dudek combined his two modes with a manifesto on poetry, in poetry. His "Functional Poetry: A Proposal" shows just how far Dudek intended to take his discursive style in verse:

> The problem, it seems to me, is simply
> the loss of ground to prose   over the centuries
> in the subject matter of poetry,
>
> and the loss of freshness in method
> as the residue of "poetic" substance
> became fossilized in decadent metre and form
>   — the coral reefs.

The limitations which he would accept would be few:

> ... some form of improvised rhythmed speech
> which is divided and shaped
>   by the run-on and end-stop system
>   of notation.[72]

Through "A Note on Metrics" and "Functional Poetry," Dudek established the mode which he has continued to support and within which he has continued to write until the present. The fact that both of these works are products of the late 1950s, and that both were published in *Delta*, says much about the value of this period in Dudek's development. *Europe*, the first lengthy example of Dudek's discursive style, was published in 1954. Although not published until 1960, *Literature and the Press* had been completed as a dissertation in 1955. Dudek's major achievement as a magazine editor, *Delta*, was begun in 1957.

The importance of *Europe* in the establishment of Dudek's style, and as an example of his devotion to Pound's poetic ideals, cannot be overestimated. As a number of critics have noted, at times begrudgingly, it was also noteworthy for its time as a statement by a young Canadian poet that he felt quite capable of escaping idyllic lakes, and even Montreal ghettos, to take all of Western civilization as his subject.

The opening section of the poem presents a problem that continues throughout. When Dudek is at his worst, his observations are facile and even banal:

> Travelling tourist class, to Europe
> out of American, Canadian cities.
> What are we going to find?
> What are we going to see?
>
> (*CP*, p. 77)

As the ship moves down the Saint Lawrence, Dudek begins to find his medium, something approximating stream-of-consciousness, often with only tenuous connections between lines. The reflections can be superficial, but at times they have a sententious and compelling quality:

> The river brings them its mixed blessings,
> other people's broken wrongs; brought its
> accumulation of dead habits,
> the racial tics of other nations.
> Prisoners, castaways, the poor, the malcontents
> came to the colonies.
> Raw matter for a raw country,
> too often wasted and withered there, unused, left to dry.
>
> (*CP*, p. 80)

When Dudek arrives in England, his observations are again a combination of the prosaic, "Ruins are beautiful" (*CP*, p. 88), and the lyrical, "The present is shaped out of the first / shaped stones, / from Stonehenge to this" (*CP*, p. 89). The uneasy relationship between his new direct style and the remnants of his overt poeticizing is at times jarring. His initial reaction to the presence of graffiti at Winchester is "an American goon / painted on the door / saying 'yak yak' to all this" (*CP*, p. 89). A few lines later, on seeing similar desecrations on the tomb of Richard Fox, he states, "They would have had no stone / to write so plainly on, if death had not offered them / its bony breast" (*CP*, p. 90).

An intriguing comment on this problem can be found in the section on the lake country. Here, when straying from broad social comment to direct observations on literature, Dudek is best able to avoid being poetical and to succeed in being convincing:

> Wordsworth has outdone Shakespeare, by making his
> poems as sizeable and safe as these mountains.
> That's why the English love him. Though I doubt
> whether many today who holiday here
> think much in passing of his name.
>
> (*CP*, p. 93)

It often seems that Dudek, the social critic, is more at home when continuing the poet's convention of reflecting on other literature or on nature. In a rather different style, but I think with a similar conviction, Dudek finds the sea to equal Wordsworth as a source of purposeful thought:

> There is something disturbing in being again on water,
> I ask the white sea
> if there is life anywhere
> as foaming, as glowing green, as this;
> if land can possibly be, or have,
> ever, all that the sea contains.
>
> (*CP*, p. 93)

Still, the majority of the poem is not devoted to either the natural or the literary, but to a continual evocation of Dudek's main theme, the importance of an individual intellectual's analysis of life. The numerous economic references have a strong resemblance to the theories of Pound, as Frye noted,[73] but they are also consistent with statements Dudek has made elsewhere, such as in *Literature and the Press*, and which Pound would have found unacceptably left-wing.[74] The essence of Dudek's position is always a liberation in which the individual is never in bondage, whether to the wealthy few or to the poor majority:

> As for democracy, it is not just the triumph
> of superior numbers,
> but that everyone, continually,
> should think and speak the truth.
> What freedom is there in being counted among the cattle?
> The first right I want is to be a man.
>
> (*CP*, p. 116)

At this point, Dudek still presents a view of the peasant which might be called sentimental socialist, but his essentially élitist tendencies are becoming more and more clear. Regardless of his continued call for democracy, his philosophy is something closer to a libertarian one. As he journeys through Italy, he observes that the mass in the modern age have little interest in the eternal verities of the past:

> I am sure the Italians would trade in Santa Croce
> (with all the bones that are in it)
> for a row of comfortable Duplex houses
> on the outskirts of Montreal.
> It's the one against the other. And where do we stand?
> We, we are not given the choice.
> We are a principle in ourselves,
> a foreign body in those suburbs;
> building something in the mind only, whose shape, dim
> and white, trembles and becomes solid sometimes —
> the one good line in a poem.
>
> (*CP*, p. 108)

The democratic urge might be there, but isolation is the guiding feeling, reinforced by the intellectual poet's royal "we."

At the end of the poem, Dudek once more returns to the Saint

Lawrence as he heads towards Montreal. As in the introduction, simplicity takes over, but this time, instead of the banal, he achieves a feeling of absolute spareness and accuracy:

> Getting started is never easy.
> We have work to do.
> Europe is behind us.
> America before us.
>
> (*CP*, p. 125)

One is reminded of Frederick Philip Grove's *A Search for America*: "Europe regards the past; America regards the future. America is an ideal and as such has to be striven for; it has to be realized in partial victories."[75] In at least this instance, Dudek's use of open verse and his simplicity of diction have gone a long way towards making stirring prose still more stirring poetry.

In some ways, *Literature and the Press* continues *Europe*'s views of the individual and his attempt to overcome economic enslavement, but it does this in a more limited realm and in a more scholarly manner, with numerous statistics and historical references. Still, at least in the published version, Dudek lays no claims to objectivity. The introduction states,

> If permanent literature is important, and if it is to regain its dominant place, it will only be after we begin to realize the dangers inherent in the machinery of modern communications, and consciously work to counteract them.[76]

The work provides parallel histories of the development of English literature and of printing. For Dudek, the mechanics of the latter suggest a constant and telling metaphor:

> The newspaper can be described as the first demonstration of the machine speaking in the new society, since the newspaper makes use of machinery for the widest possible dissemination of the printed word. (*LP*, p. 39)

Dudek sees the newspaper as more than a collective production; it is an extension of the machine. This is the writing most removed from the liberated individual.

Machine printing led to a form of writing which is governed by the needs of machinery, such as volume publication. Dudek suggests this to be the cause of a "tyranny of cash" (*LP*, p.151) which kept Thackeray and Dickens from reaching their potential as writers. In contrast, Dudek turns to Carlyle, "a study in literary integrity and in the difficulties which integrity in the modern age must find on its way" (*LP*, p.205). He maintains, "Carlyle was in the first place an artist as thinker; and in our time it is the fate of the artist, the thinker, the hero, which reveals to us the distortions of our culture" (*LP*, p.219).

There was little contemporary reaction to the publication of *Literature and the Press*, and what there was was not very favourable.[77] This is not surprising given its sloppy prose, faults in documentation, and errors in logic. It is all very well to be subjective, but Dudek's tendency to divide things into black and white left little room for the positive contributions of the wide availability of print. He also had a Procrustean way with history and historical figures. His view of Dickens is closer to the early twentieth-century denigration of him as a pulp writer than to later re-evaluations. He tends to forget that part of Carlyle which could create a persona named Diogenes Teufelsdröckh, or God-begotten Devil's dung. Dudek's Carlyle attacks the Teufelsdröckh evils of society, but there is little suggestion of the rather mad Diogenes who Carlyle hoped could supersede them.

The primary value of the book today is the light it sheds on Dudek's other, much more successful works. This is most evident with respect to *Delta*, the publication that I would see as Dudek's major contribution to Canadian culture. Dudek was not too modest to record in *Delta* the praises given by his readers, and it is difficult to disagree with them.[78] The little magazine has been an essential part of the development of contemporary Canadian poetry, and quite simply *Delta* has been the best of the bunch.

The faults Dudek displayed in *Literature and the Press* are his virtues in *Delta*. The rather egotistical and expansive generalist, whose thoughts often come in a scatter-gun, was too untameable for a volume of social history, but perfect as a little-magazine editor. As well, in *Delta* he added the care in presentation wanting in *Literature and the Press*. At least one meaning of the title — the Greek name of the letter *D* — suggests how closely the magazine was tied to its editor. In the first issue, Dudek states:

> In short, this will be something of a personal magazine, with an impersonal program. I take poetry to mean a special form of writing, rhythmic, whole, heated by imagination, but with no restrictions of subject or form placed upon it, and with the same vitality of interests that prose has: we must win back the ground we have lost to prose, and discover new ground.[79]

It was to be a magazine suitable for a Carlyle, "the artist, the thinker, the hero," who would overcome the "dangers inherent in the machinery of modern communications."

The substance of *Delta* is exactly what one might expect from Dudek. The poetry shows an eclectic selection, but most of the prose is from Dudek's pen and on Dudek's favourite subjects. He attacks the electronic media in pieces on the CBC[80] and Arthur Miller.[81] In " 'The Paperback Revolution' — Has It Guillotined Poetry?"[82] he continues to reject the possibility of valuable writing in a mass market. He gives the first glimpse of his attempt to find the poetry of realism through science:

> If we are ever going to get over the split between intelligent thinking and vacuous poetizing, however, we must do it by bridging the gap between scientific knowledge and imaginative-emotional-credencial experience.[83]

In various other pieces, Dudek pursued his search for science, and he published several other contributions on the subject, including one by D.G. Jones. Another contributor, John Van Sickle, suggested that poetry is not primarily a vehicle for ideas, but rather an "affect." Dudek's reply shows him at his argumentative best:

> Poetry as affect b.s. There is no affect without object (except in the neurotic and psychotic) and the object brings us right against science. You get your muddled ideas out of books, and bad ones (I.A. Richards on poetry as "pseudo-statement" affect-vehicle for bankrupt beliefs), where the effort is to separate the incompatibles and make absurdities coexist. There is of course a good deal of absurdity in the theory of reality propounded by science. Also, we do have a

> *language* in religion, art and poetry. Those who discover this usually forget that it is what you say with a language that matters; and you still have to ask what a religion, or an artist, has said, and whether it is true. So get to work on real thinking, creating the viable, verifiable truth.[84]

Dudek's various reviews in *Delta* show him working out his ideas on science and poetry. In "Julian Huxley, Robert Graves and the Mythologies," he suggests that mythmaking is only suitable in an age without "the descriptive abstraction": "The growth of abstract thought, and hence of science, is the invention of an efficient method of superficial analysis, which leaves the transcendental problems in suspension for a later and more careful assessment."[85] An examination of the work of the Vancouver poets leads to a decision that "...it is a form of realism, that carried to the extreme, the nadir of unmeaning, must progress ultimately, out of dissatisfaction, to a hopeful illumination."[86] In "Those Damned Visionary Poets (Les Poètes Maudits Visionnaires)," Dudek sees some Quebec writers as tending towards "a tragic submergence in the unconscious."[87]

The culmination of Dudek's explorations is found in one of the last issues of *Delta*. In "The Fallacy of Literalism and the Failing of Symbolic Interpretation," Dudek rejects the possibilities of literature as only documentation and literalism, on the one hand, or as symbol—whether myth or internal psychological vision—on the other. Imagination is essential, but it must be joined with a conscious evocation of reality:

> To relate the precision of reason and consciousness to the emotional reality of these synthetic symbols is to have the key to all seriousness and significance in art and life.
>
> Literature, then, should never be read merely as a literal depiction of reality; nor should the symbolic interpretation of literature ever suffice as evaluation or account of its nature. Symbolic reading, like realistic relevance, is only a first step in criticism; it does not provide us with any criteria of evaluation....A work of art is one man's emotional drama. It is great if it contains in its complex of artistic relations, in its sign language, the fullest expression of truth about life and the most intense and convincing vision of our

> aspirations and desires....Art is the perfect union of the real and the ideal, in the form of fiction.[88]

For Dudek, true art cannot be produced either by the mass media, the mechanical mob, or by the mythopoeists, who place all art within certain symbolic structures. Both limit the scope in which the artist can examine his personal view of reality. One is obsessed with common reality to the point of minute documentation and no exercise of imagination. Purely visionary art has the opposite problem — a free imagination, but little contact with society and the reality of general human experience. The height of art can be found only in the "perfect union" of the artistic imagination and the real society in which the artist lives.

In many ways, *Delta* as a whole is the evocation of such principles. Dudek quoted widely, with excerpts from the work of C.P. Snow, Michael Hamburger, Goethe, Thomas Love Peacock, and many others. He was willing to go beyond even the quasi-literary, as in one quotation from *The Canadian Packing House Worker.* When nuclear fear was on the rise, *Delta*, No. 20 (Feb. 1963), devoted its cover to a call for "New Roads to Peace":

> RESOLVED: That the next war should be fought on the moon.
> RESOLVED: That atomic scientists should be transferred to work on love potions.
> RESOLVED: That this poetry magazine be made required reading in all armies and military academies.

The prose was usually Dudek's, and when it was not, it was usually chosen to suit Dudek's ideology. This was not the case, however, in his selection of poetry. The most frequent contributors were those Dudek had assessed to be realists, F.R. Scott, Raymond Souster, Alden Nowlan, Al Purdy, W.W.E. Ross, Milton Acorn, and Dorothy Livesay, but some predominantly mythopoeic poets were also given significant space, D.G. Jones, Jay Macpherson, Ralph Gustafson, and the early Margaret Atwood. Perhaps still more important was *Delta*'s policy of concentrating on Canadian writers, but remaining open to all nations, with poems from the United States, Britain, Russia, China, and even Nigeria. In the case of some French and German poems, Dudek published both original and translation.

Not long after the beginning of *Delta*, Dudek published his second long meditative poem, *En México* (1958). Once again he begins with the ocean. His first words are "In waves of weariness," and he rapidly comes to "A roar of sea" (*CP*, p. 197). The interaction with the sea is wholehearted and sensual, becoming Whitmanesque in his participation with the peasants on the shore: "Sing, as we now sing!" (*CP*, p. 207). There is also a feeling for the land, but it is much more tentative:

You may hate the jungle,
its inimical insects, flies,
and the chaos of growing
everything at once;
but we return for fertility
to its moist limbs and vaginal leaves.

(*CP*, p. 203)

The attraction of nature in *En México* is stronger, in general, than in *Europe*. One might relate this to two other long poems from this period, "Keewaydin Poems" (1955) and "At Lac En Coeur" (1960). In both he seeks a tranquility and regeneration in nature but is still distanced by his humanity, both as a social and as an intellectual being. In the first, he remarks,

I am not unlike the world around me,
many and muddled, a contradictory thing,
yet like the lake water, swell with some clear
        delicious spring...
                        Shall I stand up and crow?

(*CP*, p. 138)

Five years later, Dudek is still drawn to nature, at Lac En Coeur, but he recognizes his own limitations even more: "Who thinks the living universe? / I think it but in part" (*CP*, p. 218). He concludes, however, with a hope for the idea: "Anywhere the eyebeam transects the world, a thorn / strikes with such sharpness to a thought" (*CP*, p. 219).

In *En México*, the natural world seems closer to that found in Keewaydin than at Lac En Coeur. Still, all three poems share a concern for an accommodation between nature and the idea, as expressed in this passage from *En México*:

There are degrees of beauty.
But as to what makes one flower
more to be prized than another —
we can define the elements, their order,
and what they do in the eye, or mind,
but the shaping hands are undivined.

(*CP*, p. 204)

The main distinction between this poem and "Keewaydin Poems" and "At Lac En Coeur" is that—though to a lesser degree than in *Europe* — Dudek's social observations still predominate in *En México*.

One of the most memorable passages in *En México* presents Dudek's attempt to assert the value of man and society: "Evil is in the warp and weft of reality, / but the whole cloth is good, is good" (*CP*, p. 211). At this point, he was still unwilling to cast off the unintellectual mass, but the élitist stance of one true voice crying in a mob or wilderness is becoming more clear. It is a position which shaped his view of literary traditions in *The First Person in Literature* (1967), a collection of lectures which Dudek gave on the CBC-FM series *Ideas*.

First Person is itself a contribution to a mass medium, but like Dudek's pieces in *The Gazette* [Montreal], it is very much a fifth column, with numerous attacks on the forces which make the medium possible. It presents literature as a developing liberation from dogma. Dudek maintains that in the beginning literature spoke for the values of an absolute state and an absolute religion. He sees the major change in the Romantics, among whom the Byronic hero represents the possible extension of the liberated individual writer: "It is an imagined personality built up out of elements that existed in the real life of the author..." (*FPL*, p. 15). The danger is that the writer may become obsessed with "total self-expression" (*FPL*, p. 20). The alternative is "a humane enlargement of the ego" (*FPL*, p. 21). Great artists "are great moralists, in fact, at the same time that they are egotists, and it is their extreme morality that saves them. This is, of course, an element of objectivity" (*FPL*, p. 21).

Yet, paradoxically, the most objective reality is not real enough. Dudek maintains that those writers who present simply documentary evidence leave the audience unsatisfied. The readers require the medium of the great individual artist, of whom Dudek's prime examples are Whitman, Joyce, Proust, and Pound. Dudek believes that each such artist achieves a "transcendent" reality (*FPL*, p. 44). Through his subjective visions, each communicates his own deeply personal view of reality in such a manner as to produce a corresponding, yet individually different, vision in those to whom his art is directed. Dudek states, "Science needs art to supplement its inhuman reality, its feeble metaphysics" (*FPL*, p. 56). When the powers of the individual great writer are applied to the facts of life, the science, the material, becomes transformed into something no longer inhuman. It can then inspire another individual subjective perception, that of the reader. Dudek asserts that "... the liberation from the gods, and the liberation of the individual self, to face alone the great issue of existence — working always for this time and this place, this self, to find the hidden meaning of all things — that is the great adventure" (*FPL*, p. 68).

In *Atlantis* (1967), one can judge Dudek's own contribution to the great adventure, for one is compelled to believe that Dudek sees himself in this line of great individual moderns. To many, this might seem like incredible hubris, but I think the point is, not in what Dudek sees as his achievement, but in what he sees as his purpose. His decision is the attempt; it is for others to assess his success.

The character of the poem, as Dudek sees it, is clearly presented in Michael Darling's "An Interview with Louis Dudek" (1975):

> Atlantis — the idea or concept of Atlantis came to me in mid-ocean — the mythological or symbolic word that contains what I'm talking about. Unfortunately, Ron Everson said to me, on reading the book, "I've read through three-quarters of it and haven't seen Atlantis yet." It's quite true that it isn't visible in any concrete way — it isn't even in our lives; you don't see glory or heaven anywhere, you don't see God or transcendence. And I'm not interested in taking drugs to try to experience that sort of thing — but there is something going on, in the actual, and *Atlantis* is such a meticulous, on-going, and perhaps boring poem, because it's constantly testing and seeking and trying to

> justify, and document, this particular kind of search. I am that kind of Diogenes. I'm walking through the poem, through Europe, trying to see what it is; and of course it's in great works of art that I see for a moment what I'm looking for in that poem. But I'm not looking much at works of art; I'm looking mainly at people in streets, in restaurants, in hotels, where I talk to them, and at myself and at my life. I'm trying to understand what it is that has value and meaning, to rebuild the other half of possible existence.[89]

The poem is not really different in kind from *Europe* and *En México*, but it represents a development from them. Although very far from Whitman in most ways, *Atlantis* maintains a similarity in the manifestation of the ego of the poet: "I will take it all in and wait / until like a Univac / I suddenly throw up the sum" (*CP*, p. 277). Dudek still sees the possibility of the individual poet taking the confusion of the universe and distilling a whole truth.

Dudek presents the process of taking it all in in such a manner as to suggest his immediate reactions to events and reflections as they happen:

> Voices, baggage, a girl's knee,
> and bells, distant, obscure
> Every object a word, language, the record we make
> a literal transcription,
> then a translation
> into moral, abstract meaning.
>
> Travel, to and from (the place does not matter)
> the Ding an sich in a mirror —
> Let it speak!
>
> (*CP*, p. 223)

As one might surmise from Dudek's comment in "The Fallacy of Literalism," it is that process of translation that is the core of his poetry: "You've got to make something out of what is there / and make it true / to that reality like nothing else, like no one else, in you" (*CP*, p. 236). Even with this assertion of the modern individual poet speaking, Dudek still maintains some Romantic notions about his role. He observes himself directed by "the

Angel of Poetry": "And this is somehow his good, / not mine" (*CP*, p.237).

The substance of the poetry in *Atlantis* is a search for an ideal. At the beginning, Dudek returns once more to his favourite source of inspiration:

> Like this ship leaving, gently, to silent tears
> falling all around,
> the infinite poem begins, with its power
> of a great ocean-liner greeting the waves,
> bound for the sea, its home.
>
> (*CP*, p.225)

He searches for an answer throughout Europe, particularly in art, but in the end there is only one assurance: "There is the sea. It is real" (*CP*, p.285).

One of the most important aspects of *Atlantis* is its demonstration of the coming together of Dudek's prose and poetry. His earlier poems have forms and content which reflect Dudek's critical position, but they lack the declarative polemic so often found in his prose. As the meditative poem has developed, Dudek has been able to assert his views quite directly. This is often seen in a free association of epigrammatic statements, which Dudek first demonstrated in *En México*:

> Religion is an open question.
>
> I thought, seeing the layered stones —
> how wonderful
> the pursuit of knowledge!
> When on the lettered rock-face
> appeared a skull and bones.
>
> Optimism is foolish. Life can only be
> tragic, no matter what its success.
>
> (*CP*, p.202)

By *Atlantis*, Dudek had honed his open verse structure to the point that it provides the best possible form for his type of rhetoric:

Time floats like an island
in the sea of being.
We must study
its birds and flowers as language
that tells us our past and future.
For there is no other knowledge.

Think of the idiots who want a "vision,"
having the sun-blasted world before their eyes.
It has been given!

(*CP*, p. 250)

Again, Dudek presents the necessity of realism. Yet, if this is the best medium for Dudek's message, why has the majority of his work since *Atlantis* been in prose? The answer might be found in two short lines from that poem: "I do not love my fellow men / but only citizens of Atlantis" (*CP*, p. 231). Dudek has found too few such citizens to respond to his poetry. The answer has been to emphasize his criticism and his public speaking, in an attempt to create an atmosphere in which the population of Atlantis might grow.

Reference to *Atlantis* as a medium for Dudek's message provides an ironic comment on his latest work in that most of Dudek's efforts since the 1960s have been directed against the "medium is the message" man, Marshall McLuhan, and Dudek's "Great White Whale of Canadian Criticism," Northrop Frye. To link these two critics together might seem strange, but not if one accepts Dudek's interpretation. He sees McLuhan as limiting the individual artist by extolling the power of media which are shaped by the mob. He believes that Frye limits the individual artist by forcing all literature into one critical system. The result in both cases is a devaluation of the artist as individual thinker commenting on reality.

Dudek's questions about McLuhan's analysis go back at least to *Literature and the Press*. To the extent that he labels McLuhan a proselytizer for the mass media, Dudek's opposition needs little explanation, but he goes well beyond that, as in "The Misuses of Imagination: A Rib-Roasting of Some Recent Canadian Critics" (1973):

> McLuhan is a metaphor-maker, or more precisely, since this is a big ambition, a myth-maker. The myth fails to convince, it does not apply really, but that is what it is: false prophecy, an irresponsible use of imagination. Thus, McLuhan never strictly investigates the effects of the media in any conscientious effort to find out what the actual effects are (this would be a minor project, and a doubtful one, in a psychology lab—e.g., Is the "ratio of the senses" altered by TV watching?); he merely uses his inspired guesses to project his own metaphorical order on reality, and the reasons for this are not in the media but in McLuhan himself.[90]

Thus McLuhan is a part of the same mythicizing process as Frye. In "Frye Again (but Don't Miss Souster)" (1958), the article in which the above reference to Frye as Moby Dick appears, Dudek asserts that Frye "tries to reduce the whole spirit and meaning of art to a factor of his system of classification, a mere product of 'type' and 'form,' having nothing to do with the author's mind, heart, or convictions."[91] Dudek believes that McLuhan and Frye give free rein to their imaginations and then claim the results to be systems which are scientific facts and within which art cannot help but fit.

Again, in "The Misuses of Imagination," Dudek shows his rejection of Frye's attempt to find a universally applicable analysis. He maintains that mythopoeic criticism "tries to reduce particular works to the level of a generalized concept. A myth is essentially a generalized metaphor: like all generality it obscures perception, and at worst it becomes dogma."[92] In "Northrop Frye's Untenable Position" (1963), Dudek gives the following portrait of Frye's system:

> ...the poet becomes significant to the critic, as one possessed by a Platonic reality over and above the rational and sensible consciousness of man, but he is not himself a useful thinker, because the entire form of his "central myth" is already in the hands of the critic, and each poet, as the critic's guinea pig, provides only a partial illustration of the archetypal plan.[93]

"The Psychology of Literature" (1977), the final piece in *Selected Essays and Criticism*, provides a summation of Dudek's opposition to Frye, and of his general critical stance. He asserts his respect for Frye, "probably the greatest critic of the century,"[94] but he cannot accept any all-inclusive critical system: "The source of every work of literature is in a human individual, and that individual in a particular state of mind and motivation" (p. 374). Through himself, he speaks out for that individual:

> I cannot accept that imagination is pre-programmed as "A structural power, which, left to itself, produces vigorously predictable fictions." I revolt against a view of literature that sees in it "abstract story-patterns" with "interchangeable motifs that can be counted and indexed." I oppose the tyranny of a view which claims that "mythology as a total structure, defining as it does a society's religious beliefs... is the matrix of literature, and major poetry keeps returning to it." I do not want to keep "returning"; I want to go forward. And I believe that literature does go forward, as human thought goes forward. (p. 369)

The almost obsessive use of the first person here suggests both Dudek's emotion and his belief in himself as an individual writer and thinker. His concern that art be a comment on reality would be enough to cause his attack on Frye, but the vigour of that attack is related to other factors. Dudek is an élitist and progressivist, philosophical positions which have not been generally espoused of late. He believes that society in general may have progressed. He is able to follow this progression up to the "great moderns," most particularly Pound, but he makes only tentative proposals about those who have come after.

Dudek clearly hopes that he, himself, can be seen in that line. His commitment to his role as poet can be seen in his latest long poem, *Continuation 1* (1981), which is described in the Preface as "the first book in a poem without prescribed end or conclusion."[95] In his interview with Nause and Heenan, Dudek commented,

> Yes, an infinite poem in progress, in which the main job is simply recording the words that come to you and writing them down continually in a book, and then reworking them

> —rarely, very rarely altering the position of the lines. Sometimes this may be necessary, but it should be avoided. Usually cutting out, rephrasing slightly; I have a respect for divine dictation. (p. 41)

Part of *Continuation 1* first appeared in *Collected Poetry* (1971), followed by another segment in *The Tamarack Review* (Summer 1976). Both these sections and three new ones are included in the book publication of the poem. The lack of even a general focus makes it difficult to see the work as more than a series of sententious non sequiturs, but the Preface suggests that Dudek hopes the reader will be able to find more:

> If it has an order it is an order in the nature of the mind itself, or of the world we live in, not in poetic traditions or in ideas consciously held. The very method, of course, reveals a confidence in the kinds of order implicit in the nature of things, and this is perhaps an idea surfacing, or struggling to surface, at points in the poem.

Even Dudek is not willing to let his poetic wanderings stand alone, however, and there are a number of changes in the different versions. For example, in the book, a comment on Ezra Pound becomes:

> What's the good
> of these "Conversations with God"
> There is never any hurry
> to publish
>
> (p. 15)

In the *Collected Poetry*, this passage reads:

> All good poems
> are conversations with God
> and there is never any hurry
> to publish
>
> (*CP*, p. 326)

It is tempting to see this earlier version as more of a personal comment by Dudek for Dudek, a justification for his determined striking out on his own path, regardless of a lack of public acceptance.

Continuation 1 seems to represent the logical extension of Dudek's search for the long poem, but between the publication of *Atlantis* and *Continuation 1* there have been a number of other books, which are like tangents to his central quest. *Epigrams* (1975) is a collection of one-liners, again showing Dudek's love for the sententious comment. Some have a telling thrust about them: "All success is secret. That's the secret of success" (*E*, p.34). Others are just weak attempts at humour: "If the truth didn't matter I'd say Layton is a damn good poet" (*E*, p.25). For the rest, they are mainly representations of Dudek's usual stance: "It is only through individuals that a people can be raised up" (*E*, p.39).

Whether intentional or not, a number of these pieces seem to be comments on Dudek's own career. Several point to the inadequacy of those works and writers who are most praised in Canada: "Each time Canadians discover a new poet we realize again how little they know" (*E*, p.24). Other assertions seem much more pained: "Those from whom you can least expect understanding are the other writers" (*E*, p.16). Yet in the end, Dudek seems once more assured of the validity of his position: "Better to be panned for a good book than praised for a bad one" (*E*, p.52).

Cross-Section: Poems 1940–1980 is a collection of the type often seen when a writer becomes established, what a filmmaker might call the outtakes. Dudek states in his introductory note, "These are previously unpublished poems, arranged as nearly as I can remember in the order in which they were written. I have removed a number, as the MS. developed, to bring out more clearly the evolution of form and idea."[96] Still, that evolution is not very clear, except in the broadest sense that the collection begins with rather Imagistic poetry and ends with a "Fragment of Continuum." A number of the poems reflect Dudek's usual concerns but there is nothing in either form or idea which makes a significant addition to what has been previously published.

The Preface to *Poems from Atlantis* (1980), published concurrently with *Cross-Section*, states that the same impulse lies behind both books: to resurrect what is good from the past. Dudek writes of his unpublished material: "I felt a curious gratitude for all this abundance, and a certain shame, that in the vanity of self-doubt, and in the economics of publishing, I had let so much of it lie unfinished and uncared for."[97] Although *Atlantis* had been published, he thinks it had similarly been neglected by himself and by the public. His justification for republishing a selection as *Poems from Atlantis* is that "...the real interest lies in the tinkle of each chain in the sequence." Dudek states that in making the selection he is returning the material to the various short poems with which *Atlantis* began: "The new element is a kind of serial discourse, the stream of poetic consciousness (see poem 29), while the unit poem, a poetic whole, is the more traditional and easy to recognize (as in most of the other poems)." Dudek presents this book as a sampler for the original: "I hope, however, that by separating the poems here, and offering them an independent existence, framed on the page, the reader may discover *Atlantis* and go the whole voyage."

In 1979 Dudek published *Technology and Culture*, a collection of six lectures, one from 1975 and the rest from between 1969 and 1971. Two years later, *Open Letter* published its special double issue, *Louis Dudek: Texts & Essays*. It includes an interview with Dudek and reproductions of drafts from *Europe*, *Atlantis*, and *Continuation 1*. The rest comprises reprints of a few early articles and of a number of lectures given between 1968 and the present, in general quite similar to those which appeared in *Technology and Culture*.

Of the earlier material, probably the most noteworthy is "Art, Entertainment and Religion" (1963), which provides a summation of Dudek's Arnoldian view of the potential of literature:

> Only when we have come to a serious total acceptance of life, and death, in all its manifold patterns, acceptance of the tragedy and the comedy — which means the ultimate failure of human virtue — when we have come to a grand evaluation of all the detail of existence, the joy and the suffering, not merely as nonsense and hankering after forbidden fruit, but with wholesome appreciation, reverence, when we have made this accord with our rational knowledge, only then shall we have something like the art and religion we need. Our entertainment will then be art, and art will be great entertainment.[98]

In the more contemporary material, "The Theory of the Image in Modern Poetry" provides a good assessment of the power of Imagism in the twentieth century and, by inference, in Dudek's own poetry. "The Poetry of Reason" shows the philosophy which led Davey to emphasize Dudek's rationalism in *Louis Dudek & Raymond Souster*:

> But just as interpretation is the code of criticism, so greater consciousness is written into the future of poetry and of literature in general. We can expect a poetry of reason, a poetry of greater order and rationality, when the present wave of barbarism and reaction is over and done with, and when we begin to acquire real confidence in the humane skills of our best understanding. The real problem for poetry in the future is to marry modern reason to the images of the imagination and to the emotions of men. This can be done. It will be the true poetry of intelligence, and it will be the poetry of the modern world.[99]

Both *Texts & Essays* and *Technology and Culture* are worth examination by anyone interested in Dudek, but they provide few significant variations on his past statements on realism, reason in poetry, education, technology, and modernism. Their value, as in the examples quoted here, is as a mature collection of those ideas and a synopsis of Dudek's philosophy. There is a feeling that Dudek is attempting to tie together what has been his life's work, as in the following comment, in "The Poetry of the Forties," on Layton, Souster, and himself:

> I suppose I am the third in this trio — at least the critics always mention the name. Obviously I have never reached a large public with my poetry. But this does not mean that I have not carried the program of modernism forward, alongside Layton and Souster and the others, in some way of my own. My writing has to do with a whole program of practical criticism, and with poetry on many fronts, so that no general public could take it up. But I think this is as essential a part of the liberation as any other — this work of "the militant critic" and the exploratory poet — and it must eventually have its effect on Canadian poetry.[100]

In the Preface to *Technology and Culture*, Dudek suggests that his lectures have been another part of his attempt to create an effect, on literature and on society in general:

> Therefore I trench on fields outside of literature, even outside the humanities, knowing that this is where the relevant problems lie — for literature itself — in the relation to society and to the whole of reality. Poetry is the naked self responding to these conditions; the discursive mind is a product of the will that is perhaps a bit more artificial, but it is very useful in clarifying issues; and it is a function of the mind that we should not disparage. The two may exist in the same person.[101]

Both the poet and the discursive mind continue to exist in Dudek, although little new poetry has appeared in the last few years. In his prose, he has continued the call for the free individual poet commenting on reality, but for the main part of the Canadian readership, he has not been that poet. As Dudek himself has noted, readers of poetry are few in any case, but to many for whom Layton and Atwood and Birney are immediately recognizable, Dudek is a name which draws at best a vague "I remember him." Is he deserving of more?

If Frank Davey is right about Dudek's influence on modern poetry in Canada, the answer must be yes. Still, as noted above, there are a number of American sources for the lyric with "a punchline of humour or philosophy" or "the long meditational poem." Perhaps Dudek was among the first Canadians to use them, but at present this would just make him an historical footnote.

The same would be true of his work in publishing and editing. *Delta* and the various presses with which Dudek was associated were a major part of the development of contemporary Canadian literature, but they were a factor of the 1950s and 1960s. Poets today often seem very far removed from that era and from Dudek.

The importance of Dudek as a writer must be presented in a tautology. Dudek is important because he thinks he is important. If this were true only in the sense of, say, Irving Layton, for whom importance is a statement of his ego as poet, it would not be worthy of mention. But Dudek believes himself to be important because he works within the great modern tradition. He manifests the poet as individual thinker discoursing on the problems of the world. Because of this belief, Dudek has been able to liberate himself from the limitations of the lyric to write poems which consider the whole of civilization. In high polemic, he has confronted the various schools into which Canadian poetry has tended to fall. He has consistently been the poet's champion whenever he has felt the critic becoming too strong.

Perhaps in the future, Dudek's poetry will be more highly valued than it is today. But even at present, when many question his achievements in verse, and when many find his élitist and progressivist critical stance to be anathema, his importance must be accepted. Without his work, in all directions, it might be too easy, particularly in the Canadian context, to accept literature as a drawing-room activity of little concern. Dudek's call has been constant and simple:

> The arts should be on the front page. (*E*, p. 15)

NOTES

[1]Ralph Gustafson, "Louis Dudek," in *Contemporary Poets of the English Language*, ed. Rosalie Murphy (London: St. James, 1970), p. 309.

[2]Wynne Francis, "A Critic of Life: Louis Dudek as Man of Letters," *Canadian Literature*, No. 22 (Autumn 1964), p. 7. All further references to this work appear in the text.

[3]Susan Stromberg-Stein, "A Biographical Introduction to Louis Dudek's Poetry," M.A. Thesis McGill 1977, pp. 9–11.

[4]Interview between Dudek and Susan Stromberg-Stein, 16 Oct. 1975. See Stromberg-Stein, p. 25.

[5]Frank Davey, *Louis Dudek & Raymond Souster*, Studies in Canadian Literature, No. 14 (Vancouver: Douglas & McIntyre, 1980), p. 15. All further references to this work appear in the text.

[6]Raymond Souster, Letter to Louis Dudek, 23 June 1951, as quoted by Michael Gnarowski, Contact *1952–1954: Being an Index to the Contents of* Contact, *a Little Magazine Edited by Raymond Souster,*

Together with Notes on the History and the Background of the Periodical (Montreal: Delta Canada, 1966), p. 3.

[7]Northrop Frye, rev. of *Unit of Five*, *The Canadian Forum*, May 1945, p. 48.

[8]John Nause and J. Michael Heenan, "An Interview with Louis Dudek," *The Tamarack Review*, No. 69 (Summer 1976), p. 32. All further references to this work appear in the text.

[9]Louis Dudek, "The Poetry of the Forties," *Open Letter*, 4th ser., Nos. 8–9 (Spring–Summer 1981) [*Louis Dudek: Texts & Essays*], p. 293.

[10]Louis Dudek, "Academic Literature," *First Statement*, 2, No. 8 (Aug. 1944), 17–20; rpt. in Louis Dudek, *Selected Essays and Criticism* (Ottawa: Tecumseh, 1978), p. 3.

[11]Louis Dudek, "Whitman's Barbaric Yawp," *The McGill Daily*, 11 Oct. 1940, p. 2.

[12]Paul West, "Ethos and Epic: Aspects of Contemporary Canadian Poetry," *Canadian Literature*, No. 4 (Spring 1960), pp. 7–17; rpt. in *Contexts of Canadian Criticism*, ed. Eli Mandel (Chicago: Univ. of Chicago Press, 1971), p. 207.

[13]Louis Dudek, *The First Person in Literature* (Toronto: CBC Publications, 1967), p. 60. All further references to this work (*FPL*) appear in the text.

[14]Hannah Arendt, "The Mob and the Elite," *Partisan Review*, 17 (Nov.–Dec. 1950), 816–17. Quoted in Louis Dudek, "F. R. Scott and the Modern Poets," *Northern Review*, 4, No. 2 (Dec. 1950–Jan. 1951), 4–15; rpt. in Dudek, *Selected Essays and Criticism*, p. 13.

[15]Louis Dudek, "The Theory of the Image in Modern Poetry," *Open Letter*, 4th ser., Nos. 8–9 (Spring–Summer 1981) [*Louis Dudek: Texts & Essays*], p. 267.

[16]Ezra Pound, "A Stray Document," in *Make It New* (London: Faber and Faber, 1934), p. 337. Quoted in Dudek, "The Theory of the Image in Modern Poetry," p. 267.

[17]Michael Darling, "An Interview with Louis Dudek," *Essays on Canadian Writing*, No. 3 (Fall 1975), p. 2.

[18]Louis Dudek, ed., *Dk/Some Letters of Ezra Pound* (Montreal: DC Books, 1974), p. 118. In all further references, this work is abbreviated *Dk*.

[19]Louis Dudek, *Epigrams* (Montreal: DC Books, 1975), pp. 28, 30. All further references to this work (*E*) appear in the text.

[20]See: Louis Dudek, "The Significance of Lampman," *Culture*, 18 (Sept. 1957), 277–90, rpt. in Dudek, *Selected Essays and Criticism*,

pp. 65–78; Louis Dudek, "E.J. Pratt: Poet of the Machine Age," *The Tamarack Review*, No. 6 (Winter 1958), pp. 74–80, rpt. in Dudek, *Selected Essays and Criticism*, pp. 116–21; and Dudek, "F.R. Scott and the Modern Poets."

[21]A.J.M. Smith, "On Reading Certain Poems and Epistles of Irving Layton and Louis Dudek," *The Canadian Forum*, May 1957, p. 42.

[22]*Cerberus* (Toronto: Contact, 1952), p. 13. All further references to this work appear in the text.

[23]Louis Dudek, "Layton Now and Then: Our Critical Assumptions," *Queen's Quarterly*, 63 (Summer 1956), 291–93; rpt. in Dudek, *Selected Essays and Criticism*, pp. 52–55.

[24]Louis Dudek, "Patterns of Recent Canadian Poetry," *Culture*, 19 (Dec. 1958), 399–415; rpt. in Dudek, *Selected Essays and Criticism*, p. 109.

[25]Louis Dudek, "Layton on the Carpet," *Delta*, No. 9 (Oct.–Dec. 1959), pp. 17–19; rpt. in Dudek, *Selected Essays and Criticism*, p. 136.

[26]Irving Layton, "An Open Letter to Louis Dudek," *Cataract*, 1, No. 2 (Winter 1962), n. pag.; rpt. in *Engagements: The Prose of Irving Layton*, ed. Seymour Mayne (Toronto: McClelland and Stewart, 1972), pp. 175–76.

[27]Frank Davey, "Louis Dudek," in *From There to Here: A Guide to English-Canadian Literature since 1960* (Erin, Ont.: Porcépic, 1974), p. 95.

[28]Frye, rev. of *Unit of Five*, p. 48.

[29]B.K. Sandwell, "Four Very Angry Poets in a 'Unit of Five,'" *Saturday Night*, 10 Feb. 1945, p. 21.

[30]E.K. Brown, "Letters in Canada 1944: Poetry," *University of Toronto Quarterly*, 14 (April 1945), 264.

[31]E.K. Brown, "Letters in Canada 1946: Poetry," *University of Toronto Quarterly*, 16 (April 1947), 251.

[32]A.J.M. Smith, "Turning New Leaves," rev. of *East of the City*, *The Canadian Forum*, May 1947, p. 43.

[33]Earle Birney, rev. of *East of the City, Canadian Poetry Magazine*, 10, No. 2 (Dec. 1946), 44, 45.

[34]Northrop Frye, "Letters in Canada 1952: Poetry," *University of Toronto Quarterly*, 22 (April 1953), 279; rpt. in Northrop Frye, *The Bush Garden: Essays on the Canadian Imagination* (Toronto: House of Anansi, 1971), p. 20.

[35]Margaret Heideman, "Poets and Versifiers," *Saturday Night*, 26 Nov. 1955, p. 16.

[36]Milton Wilson, "Turning New Leaves," *The Canadian Forum*, Oct. 1955, p. 162.

[37]Mona Van Duyn, "A Wide Range," *Poetry* [Chicago], 88 (1956), 330.

[38]Northrop Frye, "Letters in Canada 1955: Poetry," *University of Toronto Quarterly,* 25 (April 1956), 298; rpt in Frye, *The Bush Garden*, pp. 53–54.

[39]Wilson, p. 163.

[40]Kildare R.E. Dobbs, rev. of *The Transparent Sea*, *The Canadian Forum*, Jan. 1957, p. 238.

[41]Chester Duncan, "Poetry Chronicle," *The Tamarack Review*, No. 3 (Spring 1957), p. 82.

[42]Desmond Pacey, rev. of *Laughing Stalks* and *En México, The Fiddlehead*, No. 40 (Spring 1959), p. 50.

[43]Northrop Frye, "Letters in Canada 1958: Poetry," *University of Toronto Quarterly*, 28 (July 1959), 355; rpt. in Frye, *The Bush Garden,* p. 99.

[44]A.W. Purdy, rev. of *Laughing Stalks* and *En México*, *The Canadian Forum*, Nov. 1958, pp. 187–88.

[45]Len Gasparini, rev. of *Atlantis*, *Queen's Quarterly*, 75 (Autumn 1968), 538.

[46]Peter Stevens, "The Poetic Vocation," rev. of *Atlantis*, *Canadian Literature*, No. 39 (Winter 1969), pp. 77–78.

[47]Douglas Barbour, "Poet as Philosopher," *Canadian Literature*, No. 53 (Summer 1972), pp. 18–29; rpt. in *Poets and Critics: Essays from* Canadian Literature, *1966–1974*, ed. George Woodcock (Toronto: Oxford Univ. Press, 1974), p. 121.

[48]Dorothy Livesay, "The Sculpture of Poetry: On Louis Dudek," *Canadian Literature*, No. 30 (Autumn 1966), p. 27. All further references to this work appear in the text.

[49]Frank Davey, Introd., *Open Letter*, 4th ser., Nos. 8–9 (Spring–Summer 1981) [*Louis Dudek: Texts & Essays*], p. 7.

[50]Dudek, "The Theory of the Image in Modern Poetry," p. 281.

[51]John Robert Colombo, "Dudek: The Last of the Lot," *The Globe and Mail*, 31 Jan. 1976, p. 37.

[52]Mel Dagg, rev. of *Collected Poetry*, *The Fiddlehead*, No. 94 (Summer 1974), p. 111.

[53]Michael Hornyansky, "Letters in Canada 1971: Poetry," *University of Toronto Quarterly*, 31 (Summer 1972), 333.

[54]Dudek, "Layton on the Carpet," in *Selected Essays and Criticism*, p. 136.

[55]Cryptic [pseud.], "Lit Crit: Silence Is Essential," *The McGill Daily*, 27 Jan. 1939, p. 2.

[56]Louis Dudek, "Soliloquy of an Amoeba," *The McGill Daily*, 17 Oct. 1938, p. 2.

[57]Louis Dudek, "Improvisation," in *Collected Poetry* (Montreal: Delta Canada, 1971), p. 1. All further references to this work (*CP*) appear in the text.

[58]Pound, "A Stray Document," p. 337.

[59]Louis Dudek, "Poets of Revolt... or Reaction?" *First Statement*, 1, No. 20 (June 1943), 5.

[60]Gnarowski has been associated with Dudek for a number of years. It seems likely that his selection would be close to Dudek's own choices.

[61]Dudek, "Academic Literature," in *Selected Essays and Criticism*, p. 3.

[62]Barbour, p. 121.

[63]Dorothy Livesay, Letter, *It Needs to Be Said*, No. 5 [1975?], p. 4.

[64]Louis Dudek, "Louis Dudek Writes," *It Needs to Be Said/The Front*, 2nd ser., No. 1 [1976?], p. 2.

[65]Dudek, "F. R. Scott and the Modern Poets," in *Selected Essays and Criticism*, pp. 19–20.

[66]Louis Dudek, "Où sont les jeunes?" *Contact*, 1, No. 1 (Jan. 1952), 1; rpt. in Dudek, *Selected Essays and Criticism*, p. 25.

[67]*Twenty-four Poems* (Toronto: Contact, 1952), p. 18.

[68]Louis Dudek, rev. of *Proensa*, by Paul Blackburn, *In Cold Hell, in Thicket*, by Charles Olson, and *A Kind of Act Of*, by Robert Creeley, *CIV/n*, No. 5 (1954), pp. 23–27; rpt. in Dudek, *Selected Essays and Criticism, p.* 37.

[69]*Laughing Stalks* (Toronto: Contact, 1958), p. 77.

[70]Louis Dudek, "A Note on Metrics," *Delta*, No. 5 (Oct. 1958), pp. 15–17; rpt. in Dudek, *Selected Essays and Criticism*, p. 113.

[71]Dudek, "A Note on Metrics," in *Selected Essays and Criticism*, p. 114.

[72]Louis Dudek, "Functional Poetry: A Proposal," *Delta*, No. 8 (July 1959), pp. 1, 6.

[73]Frye, "Letters in Canada 1955: Poetry," pp. 53–54.

[74]At one point in his correspondence with Dudek, Pound asks, "and Dudek is still f equenting [sic] New Dealers.??" Dudek notes, "The little dig about New Dealers reveals how Pound saw my political position" (Dudek, *Dk*, pp. 107, 109).

[75]Frederick Philip Grove, *A Search for America: The Odyssey of an*

Immigrant (1927; rpt. Toronto: McClelland and Stewart, 1971), p. 382.

[76]Louis Dudek, *Literature and the Press: A History of Printing, Printed Media, and Their Relation to Literature* (Toronto: Ryerson-Contact, 1960), p. 11. All further references to this work (*LP*) appear in the text.

[77]A good example of this is Tony Emery, rev. of *Literature and the Press*, *Canadian Literature*, No. 9 (Summer 1961), pp. 62–64.

[78]James Boyer May, the editor of *Trace: The Guide to Little Magazines*, called Dudek "the No. 1 editor in the English-language field today. We were trying to settle on a truly edited periodical. I could think of but one" (James Boyer May, Letter, *Delta*, No. 9 [Oct.–Dec. 1959], p. 12).

[79]Louis Dudek, "Why a New Poetry Magazine," *Delta*, No. 1 (Oct. 1957), p. 3.

[80]Louis Dudek, "Talking Doorknobs," *Delta*, No. 8 (July 1959), pp. 22–23.

[81]Louis Dudek, "Arthur Miller and 'The Misfits,' " *Delta*, No. 15 (Aug. 1961), pp. 26–27.

[82]*Delta*, No. 14 (March 1961), pp. 5–7.

[83]Louis Dudek, "Psychology, Evolution and Sex," *Delta*, No. 2 (Jan. 1958), p. 18.

[84]Louis Dudek, "Reply," *Delta*, No. 14 (March 1961), p. 13.

[85]*Delta*, No. 4 (July 1958), p. 9.

[86]Louis Dudek, " 'Things' in Space: Mystic Missiles, Flying Sorcerers, Etc.: A Valedictory Article," *Delta*, No. 25 (Nov. 1965), p. 19.

[87]*Delta*, No. 18 (June 1962), pp. 5–6; rpt. in Dudek, *Selected Essays and Criticism*, p. 166.

[88]*Delta*, No. 24 (Dec. 1964), pp. 21–25; rpt. in Dudek, *Selected Essays and Criticism*, p. 185.

[89]Darling, pp. 13–14.

[90]Louis Dudek, "The Misuses of Imagination: A Rib-Roasting of Some Recent Canadian Critics," *The Tamarack Review*, No. 60 (Oct. 1973), pp. 51–67; rpt. in Dudek, *Selected Essays and Criticism*, p. 316.

[91]*Delta*, No. 5 (Oct. 1958), p. 27.

[92]Dudek, "The Misuses of Imagination," in *Selected Essays and Criticism*, p. 311.

[93]*Delta*, No. 22 (Oct. 1963), pp. 23–27; rpt. in Dudek, *Selected Essays and Criticism*, p. 177.

[94]Louis Dudek, "The Psychology of Literature," *Canadian Literature*, No. 72 (Spring 1977), pp. 5–20; rpt. in Dudek, *Selected Essays and*

Criticism, p.362. All further references to this work appear in the text.

[95]Louis Dudek, Preface, *Continuation 1* (Montreal: Véhicule, 1981), [p.7]. All further references to this work appear in the text.

[96]Louis Dudek, Introd., *Cross-Section: Poems 1940–1980* (Toronto: Coach House, 1980), [p.5].

[97]Louis Dudek, Preface, *Poems from Atlantis* (Ottawa: Golden Dog, 1980), n. pag.

[98]Louis Dudek, "Art, Entertainment and Religion," *Queen's Quarterly*, 70 (Autumn 1963), 411–30; rpt. in *Open Letter*, 4th ser., Nos. 8–9 (Spring–Summer 1981) [*Louis Dudek: Texts & Essays*], p.180.

[99]Louis Dudek, "The Poetry of Reason," *The English Quarterly*, 3, No. 2 (Summer 1970), 5–14; rpt. in *Open Letter*, 4th ser., Nos. 8–9 (Spring–Summer 1981) [*Louis Dudek: Texts & Essays*], p.211.

[100]Dudek, "The Poetry of the Forties," p.296.

[101]Louis Dudek, Preface, *Technology and Culture: Six Lectures* (Ottawa: Golden Dog, 1979), p.vii.

SELECTED BIBLIOGRAPHY

Primary Sources

Books

Dudek, Louis, et al. *Unit of Five*. Ed. Ronald Hambleton. Toronto: Ryerson, 1944.

———. *East of the City.* Toronto: Ryerson, 1946.

———, and Irving Layton, eds. *Canadian Poems 1850–1952*. Toronto: Contact, 1952.

———, Irving Layton, and Raymond Souster. *Cerberus*. Toronto: Contact, 1952.

———. *The Searching Image*. Ryerson Poetry Chap-Book, No. 147. Toronto: Ryerson, 1952.

———. *Twenty-four Poems*. Toronto: Contact, 1952.

———. *Europe*. Toronto: Laocoön (Contact), 1954.

———. *The Transparent Sea*. Toronto: Contact, 1956.

———. *En México*. Toronto: Contact, 1958.

———. *Laughing Stalks*. Toronto: Contact, 1958.

———. *Literature and the Press: A History of Printing, Printed Media, and Their Relation to Literature*. Toronto: Ryerson-Contact, 1960.

———, ed. *Poetry of Our Time: An Introduction to Twentieth-Century Poetry Including Modern Canadian Poetry*. Toronto: Macmillan, 1965.

———. *Atlantis*. Montreal: Delta Canada, 1967.

———. *The First Person in Literature*. Toronto: CBC Publications, 1967.

———, and Michael Gnarowski, eds. *The Making of Modern Poetry in Canada: Essential Articles on Contemporary Canadian Poetry in English*. Toronto: Ryerson, 1967.

———. *Collected Poetry.* Montreal: Delta Canada, 1971.

———, ed. *All Kinds of Everything: Worlds of Poetry.* Toronto: Clarke, Irwin, 1973.

———, ed. *Dk/Some Letters of Ezra Pound*. Montreal: DC Books, 1974.

———. *Epigrams*. Montreal: DC Books, 1975.

———. *Selected Poems*. Ottawa: Golden Dog, 1975.

———. *Selected Essays and Criticism*. Ottawa: Tecumseh, 1978.

———. *Technology and Culture: Six Lectures*. Ottawa: Golden Dog, 1979.

———. *Cross-Section: Poems 1940–1980*. Toronto: Coach House, 1980.

———. *Poems from Atlantis*. Ottawa: Golden Dog, 1980.

———. *Continuation I*. Montreal: Véhicule, 1981.

———. *Louis Dudek: Texts & Essays* [*Open Letter*, 4th ser. Nos. 8–9 (Spring–Summer 1981)]. Ed. Frank Davey and bpNichol.

Contributions to Periodicals

Dudek, Louis. "Soliloquy of an Amoeba." *The McGill Daily,* 17 Oct. 1938, p. 2.

———. "Whitman's Barbaric Yawp." *The McGill Daily*, 11 Oct. 1940, p. 2.

———. "Geography, Politics, and Poetry." *First Statement*, 1, No. 16 (April 1943), 2–3.

———. "Poets of Revolt...or Reaction?" *First Statement*, 1, No. 20 (June 1943), 3–5.

———. "Academic Literature." *First Statement*, 2, No. 8 (Aug. 1944), 17–20. Rpt. in *Selected Essays and Criticism*. Ottawa: Tecumseh, 1978, pp. 1–3.

———. "F. R. Scott and the Modern Poets." *Northern Review*, 4, No. 2 (Dec. 1950–Jan. 1951), 4–15. Rpt. in *Selected Essays and Criticism*. Ottawa: Tecumseh, 1978, pp. 11–23.

———. "Où sont les jeunes?" *Contact*, 1 No. 1 (Jan. 1952), 1 Rpt. in *Selected Essays and Criticism*. Ottawa: Tecumseh, 1978, pp. 24–26.

———. Rev. of *Proensa*, by Paul Blackburn, *In Cold Hell, in Thicket*, by Charles Olson, and *A Kind of Act Of*, by Robert Creeley. *CIV/n*, No. 5 (1954), pp. 23–27. Rpt. in *Selected Essays and Criticism*. Ottawa: Tecumseh, 1978, pp. 33–38.

———. "Layton Now and Then: Our Critical Assumptions." *Queen's Quarterly*, 63 (Summer 1956), 291–93. Rpt. in *Selected Essays and Criticism*. Ottawa: Tecumseh, 1978, pp. 52–55.

———. "The Significance of Lampman." *Culture*, 18 (Sept. 1957), 277–90. Rpt. in *Selected Essays and Criticism*. Ottawa: Tecumseh, 1978, pp. 65–78.

———. "Why a New Poetry Magazine." *Delta*, No. 1 (Oct. 1957), p. 3.

———. "Psychology, Evolution and Sex." *Delta*, No. 2 (Jan. 1958), pp. 17–19.

———. "Julian Huxley, Robert Graves and the Mythologies." *Delta*, No. 4 (July 1958), pp. 8–9.

———. "A Note on Metrics." *Delta*, No. 5 (Oct. 1958), pp. 15–17. Rpt. in *Selected Essays and Criticism*. Ottawa: Tecumseh, 1978, pp. 111–15.

———. "Frye Again (but Don't Miss Souster)." *Delta*, No. 5 (Oct. 1958), pp. 26–27.

———. "Patterns of Recent Canadian Poetry." *Culture*, 19 (Dec. 1958), 399–415. Rpt. in *Selected Essays and Criticism*. Ottawa: Tecumseh, 1978, pp. 94–110.

———. "E. J. Pratt: Poet of the Machine Age." *The Tamarack Review*, No. 6 (Winter 1958), pp. 74–80. Rpt. in *Selected Essays and Criticism*. Ottawa: Tecumseh, 1978, pp. 116–21.

———. "Functional Poetry: A Proposal." *Delta*, No. 8 (July 1959), pp. 1–7.

———. "Talking Doorknobs." *Delta*, No. 8 (July 1959), pp. 22–23.

———. "Layton on the Carpet." *Delta*, No. 9 (Oct.–Dec. 1959), pp. 17–19. Rpt. in *Selected Essays and Criticism*. Ottawa: Tecumseh, 1978, pp. 136–40.

———. " 'The Paperback Revolution' — Has It Guillotined Poetry?" *Delta*, No. 14 (March 1961), pp. 5–7.

———. "Reply." *Delta*, No. 14 (March 1961), p. 13.

———. "Arthur Miller and 'The Misfits.' " *Delta*, No. 15 (Aug. 1961), pp. 26–27.

———. "Those Damned Visionary Poets (Les Poètes Maudits Visionnaires)." *Delta*, No. 18 (June 1962), pp. 5–6. Rpt. in *Selected Essays and Criticism*. Ottawa: Tecumseh, 1978, pp. 166–67.

———. "Art, Entertainment and Religion." *Queen's Quarterly*, 70 (Autumn 1963), 411–30. Rpt. in *Open Letter*, 4th ser., Nos. 8–9 (Spring–Summer 1981) [*Louis Dudek: Texts & Essays*], pp. 167–80.

———. "Northrop Frye's Untenable Position." *Delta*, No. 22 (Oct. 1963), pp. 23–27. Rpt. in *Selected Essays and Criticism*. Ottawa: Tecumseh, 1978, pp. 175–79.

———. "The Fallacy of Literalism and the Failing of Symbolic Interpretation." *Delta*, No. 24 (Dec. 1964), pp. 21–25. Rpt. in *Selected Essays and Criticism.* Ottawa: Tecumseh, 1978, pp. 180–85.

———. " 'Things' in Space: Mystic Missiles, Flying Sorcerers, Etc.: A Valedictory Article." *Delta*, No. 25 (Nov. 1965), pp. 8–21.

———. "The Poetry of Reason." *The English Quarterly*, 3, No. 2 (Summer 1970), 5–14. Rpt. in *Open Letter*, 4th ser., Nos. 8–9 (Spring–Summer 1981) [*Louis Dudek: Texts & Essays*], pp. 201–11.

———. "The Misuses of Imagination: A Rib-Roasting of Some Recent Canadian Critics." *The Tamarack Review*, No. 60 (Oct. 1973), pp. 51–67. Rpt. in *Selected Essays and Criticism.* Ottawa: Tecumseh, 1978, pp. 304–19.

———. "Louis Dudek Writes." *It Needs to Be Said/The Front*, 2nd ser., No. 1 [1976?], p. 2.

———. "The Psychology of Literature." *Canadian Literature*, No. 72 (Spring 1977), pp. 5–20. Rpt. in *Selected Essays and Criticism.* Ottawa: Tecumseh, 1978, pp. 362–80.

———. "The Poetry of the Forties." *Open Letter*, 4th ser., Nos. 8–9 (Spring–Summer 1981) [*Louis Dudek: Texts & Essays*], pp. 287–99.

———. "The Theory of the Image in Modern Poetry." *Open Letter*, 4th ser., Nos. 8–9 (Spring–Summer 1981) [*Louis Dudek: Texts & Essays*], pp. 263–82.

Secondary Sources

Barbour, Douglas. "Poet as Philosopher." *Canadian Literature*, No. 53 (Summer 1972), pp. 18–29. Rpt. in *Poets and Critics: Essays from* Canadian Literature, *1966–1974*. Ed. George Woodcock. Toronto: Oxford Univ. Press, 1974, pp. 110–22.

Birney, Earle. Rev. of *East of the City. Canadian Poetry Magazine*, 10, No. 2 (Dec. 1946), 45–46.

Brown, E. K. Rev. of *Unit of Five.* In "Letters in Canada 1944: Poetry." *University of Toronto Quarterly*, 14 (April 1945), 264.

———. Rev. of *East of the City*. In "Letters in Canada 1946: Poetry." *University of Toronto Quarterly*, 16 (April 1947), 251.

Colombo, John Robert. "Dudek: The Last of the Lot." *The Globe and Mail*, 31 Jan. 1976, p. 37.

Cryptic [pseud.] "Lit Crit: Silence Is Essential." *The McGill Daily,* 27 Jan. 1939, p. 2.

Dagg, Mel. Rev. of *Collected Poetry. The Fiddlehead*, No. 94 (Summer 1974), pp. 111–16.

Darling, Michael. "An Interview with Louis Dudek." *Essays on Canadian Writing*, No. 3 (Fall 1975), pp. 2–14.

Davey, Frank. "Louis Dudek." In *From There to Here: A Guide to English-Canadian Literature since 1960*. Erin, Ont.: Porcépic, 1974, pp. 92–97.

———. *Louis Dudek & Raymond Souster.* Studies in Canadian Literature, No. 14. Vancouver: Douglas & McIntyre, 1980.

———, introd. *Open Letter*, 4th ser., Nos. 8-9 (Spring–Summer 1981) [*Louis Dudek: Texts & Essays*], pp. 7–8.

Dobbs, Kildare R.E. Rev. of *The Transparent Sea. The Canadian Forum*, Jan. 1957, p. 238.

Duncan, Chester. Rev. of *The Transparent Sea.* In "Poetry Chronicle." *The Tamarack Review*, No. 3 (Spring 1957), pp. 82–83.

Emery, Tony. Rev. of *Literature and the Press. Canadian Literature*, No. 9 (Summer 1961), pp. 62–64.

Francis, Wynne. "A Critic of Life: Louis Dudek as Man of Letters." *Canadian Literature*, No. 22 (Autumn 1964), pp. 5–23.

Frye, Northrop. Rev. of *Unit of Five. The Canadian Forum*, May 1945, p. 48.

———. Rev. of *Cerberus.* In "Letters in Canada 1952: Poetry." *University of Toronto Quarterly*, 22 (April 1953), 278–79. Rpt. in his *The Bush Garden: Essays on the Canadian Imagination.* Toronto: House of Anansi, 1971, pp. 20–22.

———. Rev. of *Europe*. In "Letters in Canada 1955: Poetry." *University of Toronto Quarterly*, 25 (April 1956), 298-99. Rpt. in his *The Bush Garden: Essays on the Canadian Imagination.* Toronto: House of Anansi, 1971, pp. 53–54.

———. Rev. of *En México*. In "Letters in Canada 1958: Poetry." *University of Toronto Quarterly*, 28 (July 1959), 354–55. Rpt. in his *The Bush Garden: Essays on the Canadian Imagination.* Toronto: House of Anansi, 1971, pp. 98–99.

Gasparini, Len. Rev. of *Atlantis. Queen's Quarterly*, 75 (Autumn 1968), 538–39.

Goldie, Terence William. "Louis Dudek: A Study of a Developing Critical Position." M.A. Thesis Carleton 1975.

Gustafson, Ralph. "Louis Dudek." In *Contemporary Poets of the English Language.* Ed. Rosalie Murphy. London: St. James, 1970, pp. 308–10.

Heenan, J.M.H. "The Voice of Order in Louis Dudek's *Collected Poetry.*" *Inscape*, 11, No. 2 (Spring 1974), 41–47.

Heideman, Margaret. "Poets and Versifiers." Rev. of *Europe. Saturday Night*, 26 Nov. 1955, pp. 16–17.

Hornyansky, Michael. Rev. of *Collected Poetry.* In "Letters in Canada 1971: Poetry." *University of Toronto Quarterly*, 41 (Summer 1972), 332–33.

Layton, Irving. "An Open Letter to Louis Dudek." *Cataract*, 1, No. 2 (Winter 1962), n. pag. Rpt. in *Engagements: The Prose of Irving Layton.* Ed. Seymour Mayne. Toronto: McClelland and Stewart, 1972, pp. 175–76.

Livesay, Dorothy. "The Sculpture of Poetry: On Louis Dudek." *Canadian Literature*, No. 30 (Autumn 1966), pp. 26–35.

———. Letter. *It Needs to Be Said*, No. 5 [1975?], p. 4.

May, James Boyer. Letter. *Delta*, No. 9 (Oct.–Dec. 1959), pp. 11–12.

Nause, John, and J. Michael Heenan. "An Interview with Louis Dudek." *The Tamarack Review*, No. 69 (Summer 1976), pp. 30–43.

Pacey, Desmond. Rev. of *Laughing Stalks* and *En México. The Fiddlehead*, No. 40 (Spring 1959), pp. 50–51.

Purdy, A.W. Rev. of *Laughing Stalks* and *En México. The Canadian Forum*, Nov. 1958, pp. 187–88.

Sandwell, B.K. "Four Very Angry Poets in a 'Unit of Five.' " *Saturday Night*, 10 Feb. 1945, p. 21.

Smith A.J.M. Rev. of *East of the City.* In "Turning New Leaves." *The Canadian Forum*, May 1947, pp. 42–43.

———. "On Reading Certain Poems and Epistles of Irving Layton and Louis Dudek." *The Canadian Forum*, May 1957, pp. 41–42.

Stevens, Peter. "The Poetic Vocation." Rev. of *Atlantis. Canadian Literature*, No. 39 (Winter 1969), pp. 77–78.

Stromberg-Stein, Susan. "A Biographical Introduction to Louis Dudek's Poetry." M.A. Thesis McGill 1977.

Van Duyn, Mona. "A Wide Range." Rev. of *Europe. Poetry* [Chicago], 88 (1956), 329–30.

Wenek, Karol W.J. *Louis Dudek: A Check-List.* Ottawa: Golden Dog, 1975.

———. "Louis Dudek's Acropolis of Words: Towards the New Democratic Age." M.A. Thesis Carleton 1976.

West, Paul. "Ethos and Epic: Aspects of Contemporary Canadian Poetry." *Canadian Literature*, No. 4 (Spring 1960), pp. 7–17. Rpt. in

Contexts of Canadian Criticism. Ed. Eli Mandel. Chicago: Univ. of Chicago Press, 1971, pp. 206–15.

Wilson, Milton. Rev. of *Europe*. In "Turning New Leaves." *The Canadian Forum*, Oct. 1955, pp. 162–63.